Sheffield Orchid Congress
Ranmoor House. 1982.

Beryl Lavell with Love.
from George xxx

The International Book of

ORCHIDS

The International Book of
ORCHIDS

P. Francis Hunt

Marshall Cavendish London & New York

Published by Marshall Cavendish Books Limited
58 Old Compton Street
London WIV 5PA

First printing 1979

Printed in Italy

© Marshall Cavendish Limited 1979

ISBN 0 85685 451 4

Introduction

More than any other group of flowering plants, orchids have acquired a reputation for glamour and mystery. This is explained, in part, by the vast range of their flower shapes, colours and smells and the specialization of their botanical features. In addition, the tropical origins of many species have lent them a highly charged exoticism, though even the more modest temperate species have their own quiet mystery. In accounting for the orchid's public image, one should not underestimate the part played by the early nurseries: sending collectors on hazardous expeditions to scour forests for unknown species and later exploiting the remarkable readiness of orchids to cross in producing the spectacular modern hybrids.

Despite the fascination orchids exercise, there is much ignorance and misunderstanding concerning them. In writing *The International Book of Orchids*, it has been the author's aim to introduce plant lovers to both the botany and horticulture of orchids, in the belief that a true understanding of these plants depends on recognizing the relationship between these two aspects.

In a book of this scale, it would be impossible to cover comprehensively the 60,000 or more different plants, species and hybrids, that belong to the orchid family. Nor is there the scope to deal with all botanical details or every aspect of cultivation. But the author will have achieved his aim if readers feel they want to extend even further their knowledge of this group of plants which, all glamour and mystery aside, are among the most remarkable in the plant kingdom.

Contents

Where to Find out About Orchids

Orchids for the Amateur Grower

The Nature of Orchids

Introduction

In the last 150 years we have discovered a lot about the nature of orchids, but these advances have been of a physical and chemical character and we are little nearer to understanding the mystique that has surrounded these plants for centuries.

Today research is continuing into orchids' gross morphology (the branch of biology that deals with a plant's form and the factors that influence it), as well as the anatomy of their vegetative and floral parts and the complex physiology involved in their pollination, fertilization and germination mechanisms. Considerable advances have been made recently into determining more accurately the chemical constitution of orchids and the extent to which this varies from species to species, a study called chemotaxonomy. The microscopic and specifically distinct features of their pollen and the behaviour of their genetic material during breeding are two areas in which much investigation has been carried out, benefiting not only scientists but the breeders and growers as well. This knowledge has been gained by studying a great variety of orchids, both specimens collected in the wild and greenhouse plants, but research into any group of living things extends equally to determining the range of forms found within that group. The question of how many different orchids there are to be found in the world has exercised men's minds since at least the middle ages. Now that most of the earth's surface has been explored and most of the larger plants have been collected at least once, and examined, we can recognize at least 18,000 different species of orchids. This total is certainly not final as many areas have never been thoroughly searched for smaller plants and, all the time, research into already collected and preserved plant specimens reveals small, technical differences that, nevertheless, are consistent and indicate that two species are involved rather than a single one. However, in some cases, botanical opinion has changed and two or more species, formerly considered distinct, are now treated as but one species.

Orchids are very remarkable plants in many ways and one of their most startling characteristics is the ease with which they hybridize or can be induced to hybridize by man. In attempts to improve upon the great variation found in nature's 18,000 species, orchid breeders have succeeded in producing tens of thousands of cross-bred hybrids and this number is being added to by at least 150 new hybrids every month.

We know much about the structure and functioning of orchids and about their variation in shape, size and colour and we know fairly well which orchids grow in each country, but our knowledge about *how* they grow in the wild is still very limited. The questions still to be answered concern their detailed preferences for soil, water and climate and their relationships with other plants and with the insects that pollinate and visit their flowers. The science of ecology, which deals with living things and their integration with all other living and non-living things in their surrounding environment, applies to orchids as well as to all other plants and animals. Orchid ecology is very much in its infancy except that we know that the relationships between man and orchids are often seriously detrimental to the orchids' well-being!

Man's relationship to orchids can be merely physical, as when they are grown for commercial sale; it can be purely aesthetic, such as when man is confronted with a picture of an orchid or a wedding bouquet or corsage of orchid flowers; or it can be

The fascination of exotic orchids soon led European nurserymen to experiment with breeding.
Phragmipedium *Grande, an artificial hybrid between two tropical American* species, P. caudatum *and* P. longifolium, *was first raised at the famous Veitch nursery in 1881. The plate is reproduced from Sander's* Reichenbachia, *a much sought after late Victorian series of orchid colour-plate books.*

both material and emotional, for example, when a gardener tends orchid plants in a greenhouse so as to produce flowers during the darkest days of winter.

Over the ages man has considered orchids with a paradoxical mixture of reverence, fear, idolatry and utility. Reverence for the fragile beauty of their flowers has expressed itself when orchids have been used as the basic motif for a primitive craft object, or latterly, for fabric and wall-covering design. Fear of orchids is unfounded on a scientific basis but the weirdly bat-shaped flowers of some species, the pseudo-carnivorous habits of some pouch-flowered plants and the monkey- or lizard-like lip of relatively humble European species are good reasons for understanding how the fear first arose. Idolatry, or as the dictionary says 'devout admiration', is easier to understand, such as when the delicately-coloured, perfectly-proportioned and · exquisitely-perfumed floral creations from a top orchid-breeding nursery are compared to a woman with the same qualities! It seems churlish to point out that to refer to a lady as 'orchidaceous' is really very insulting as the English word 'orchid' is directly derived from the Greek word for a testicle in allusion to the appearance of the paired tubers of certain European orchids.

The last quality, that of utility, meaning usefulness and profitability, refers to the considerable monetary value attached to orchid plants for a variety of reasons. In the last century rich patrons sponsored plant-collecting expeditions to search out orchids and export them to Europe to grow in their own greenhouses, and the cost of each plant that survived the rigours of collection in a tropical country, transport to the coast and on a ship to Belgium, England or France, and the completely artificial and usually quite incorrect and unsuitable conditions of the greenhouse must have been very high. Later in that century orchids were imported for commercial sale, and in order to recoup the costs incurred in their procuration they were auctioned. The exotic climes which they invoked made them realize fantastically high prices, often hundreds of guineas. Even today the latest hybrids are sold at similarly high prices, but modern methods of plant reproduction have greatly reduced the cost of the older and usually well-tried plants which any enthusiast can grow if he has the right greenhouse and

money to heat it to an adequate temperature.

It is surprising that after extolling the qualities and mentioning the other features of orchids one cannot be equally forthcoming over their usefulness to man. Despite much research and observation, the only orchids of value to man, other than in the floricultural trade, are *Vanilla planifolia*, which is the source of the popular flavouring essence Vanillin, and the seeds of certain Australian species which are reputed to have been used as oral contraceptives.

The intention of this book is to show that orchids, although unique products of creation, require their myths to be separated from their realities. The mystique that first draws the enthusiast to orchids will always be there, but every reader can learn much, and himself contribute to a better understanding of these fascinating plants.

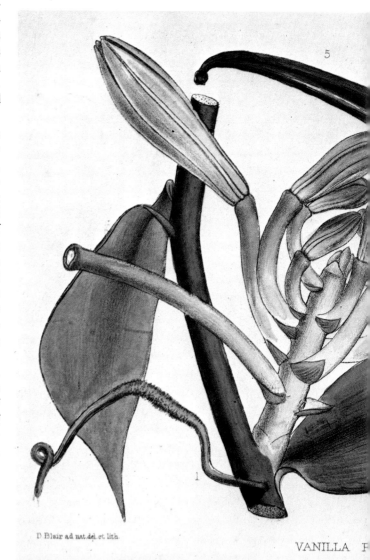

Orchids have not been widely exploited except as decorative plants. However, the Mexican species Vanilla planifolia *is now grown in many tropical countries, especially in the Malagasay Republic, as the commercial source of the flavouring vanillin.*

D. Blair ad nat.del.et lith.

VANILLA P

Botanical features

It is not only the bizarrely shaped and coloured flowers of many species that puts orchids in a special category among living things. Nearly all features of the family are botanically unique.

Seeds

As with all flowering plants, orchids arise from seeds but the characteristic that makes orchid seeds so unusual is their very small size. Millions of seeds weigh less than 25g (1 oz) but a single fertilized flower spike with perhaps twenty capsules can produce nearly a million seeds. The seeds vary from genus to genus but all are very small and consist of a very few cells forming a more or less undifferentiated embryo with virtually no food reserves at all. To enable orchid seeds to germinate successfully to produce viable seedlings the food for this is obtained, by the orchid, from a fungus with which it grows in association.

In the early days of orchid growing, success with the germination of orchid seeds was very limited, it being purely chance if the right species of fungus was around to provide the nutrients necessary. However, some species always seemed to have better seed germination rates than others, and it is felt by many growers that fungal spores are normally present on the seeds of some of these species. Considerable success is more or less guaranteed if the seeds are sown on the soil in which an orchid plant has been growing, and even greater success is assured if the seeds are sown around the base of a growing orchid plant.

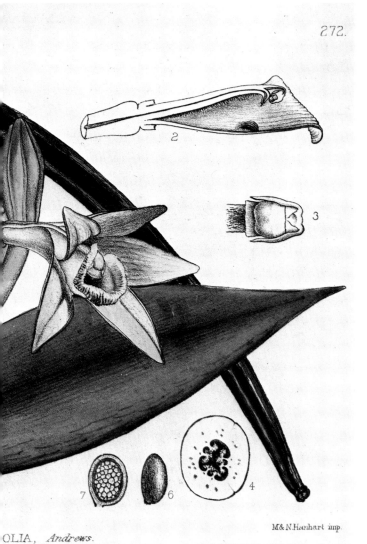

272.

OLIA, *Andrews.*

M & N. Hanhart imp.

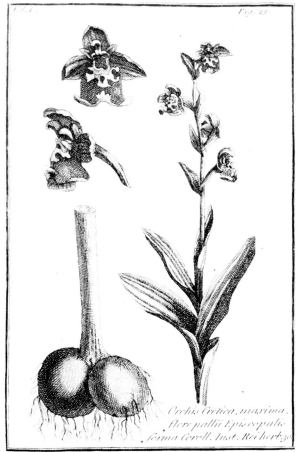

Orchis Cretica, maxima, flore pallii Episcopalis, forma Corell. Inst. Rei herb.30

Above : this early illustration shows the testiculate root tubers typical of Orchis *and most* Ophrys *species. Although once called* Orchis cretica, *this orchid is a true* Ophrys.

Today most orchid growers and breeders do not rely on chance. They germinate orchid seeds in a specially prepared sterile culture medium, usually jelly-based, in which the food that would be provided by the fungus is added as a series of chemicals. The novice orchid grower is sometimes frightened by the apparent complexity and seemingly ritualistic preparation required for this 'asymbiotic' culture of orchid seeds, but it is really very simple providing the two virtues of cleanliness and patience are your features!

Patience is necessary not only when sowing orchid seeds but also when awaiting the results of the sowing. The ripening of the seed in an orchid capsule can take up to eighteen months from pollination to seed dispersal and the germination period from sowing to the appearance of living plantlets can be equally long. To produce a flowering orchid plant from cross-pollinating two plants favoured as parents can take as long as seven years, as the time from germination to flowering can be four years. Experimentation among orchid breeders with new culture media and strictly controlled conditions has reduced this total time but three years seems to be the minimum so far achieved. It is the time involved and the cost of experimentation that make orchid plants usually more expensive than other greenhouse or outdoor decorative plants.

The seed just fertilized and the seed just about to germinate are somewhat similar in their features and this has led to experimentation to germinate freshly fertilized 'green' seeds, thus obviating the time for seed ripening and the unripening before germination. A further refinement of this process is to excise the unripened and freshly-fertilized embryos and culture them in a specially prepared nutrient medium.

This association with fungi is not confined to the germination and early development stages but continues throughout the life of most, if not all, orchids. In a mature orchid plant the fungus is found associated with nearly all tissues except the flowers but is usually concentrated in the roots.

Roots

Orchids grow in a wide range of habitats and, as with many other plants, they have developed an equally wide range of plant types to cope with the varying demands of these habitats. However, orchids are almost unique in that it is their roots that have developed in different ways whereas in most plants it is only the stems and leaves that have become modified. As a broad generalization, orchids can be divided into terrestrials, which are those plants which grow in the soil, and epiphytes, which–although not parasites–live on other plants for anchorage and to obtain an advantageous position for sunlight. About half of the total number of orchid species are epiphytes but they are confined to the tropical and sub-tropical zones and are usually found in the tropical rain forests of the equatorial regions and the evergreen mist jungles further north and south.

Opposite : despite new developments in orchid-breeding techniques, transplanting seedlings is still a time-consuming activity. In this early commercial nursery, seedlings have been *raised in community pots kept under bell-jars to maintain a humid atmosphere.*

Above : Aerial roots are typical of all epiphytic orchids. They are characterized by the green absorbent tip and the dull greyish white velamen-covered main length.

Rangaëris amaniensis is a commonly cultivated tropical East African species, closely related to the very popular Aërangis *species.*

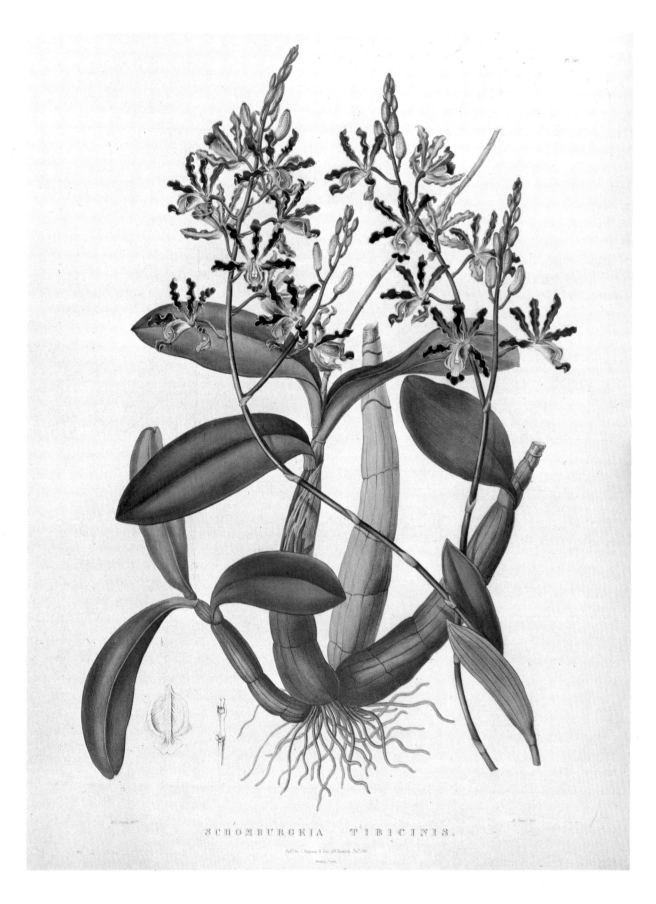

SCHOMBURCKIA TIBICINIS.

Perched on the uppermost branches of a tree or occasionally on a moss-covered rock, epiphytes are subjected to extremes of sunshine, wind, rain and drought and have developed a series of modifications to their leaves, stems and roots to cope with these particular environmental conditions. The roots have had to develop in a very special way as they are either pressed close to the bark of the host tree or dangle in the air, in neither case being protected by a covering of soil. These aerial roots are usually relatively long, sparsely branched, often tangled and coloured grey or greenish-white. They are much thicker than one would expect for relatively small plants, and this thickness is made up of an extra layer of cells around the central core of the root. Basically, this layer of dead cells, called the velamen, acts as an insulating 'water jacket' protecting the vital tissues of the active root from excessive light, heat and drought. In the early days of orchid study it was thought that the velamen envelope absorbed water from the atmosphere and conducted it into the root but we now know that water and the nutrients dissolved in it, such as sulphates, phosphates and nitrates, are absorbed only through the green apex of each root. This apex is full of rapidly dividing and very active cells, which can easily absorb the water and other substances.

It is very important when growing epiphytic orchids that their aerial roots are not immersed in soil and the natural conditions should be simulated as far as possible. To this end, epiphytic orchids are usually grown on pieces of bark, rafts of fibre or open lath baskets or, if grown in conventional flower pots, the potting medium is a mixture of osmunda fibre, sphagnum or bark, although of course most growers have their own special additives used both to reduce the cost and increase the efficiency of the medium.

The roots of orchids, in most species, arise at the base of the stem but with many epiphytic species they can arise at any position along the stem and can be above or below a leaf or an inflorescence.

Pseudobulbs

Orchid stems can be very long and wiry or they can be bamboo-like, but in many tropical species, both epiphytic and terrestrial, they are swollen for all or part of their length. These swollen stems are called pseudobulbs and their particular shape, size and arrangement can be a reliable guide to identification. Water and nutrient storage is the main function of pseudobulbs, and they often form the main perennating organ carrying the plant through unfavourable periods. Generally the pseudobulb occurs at the base of the stem but with some genera, such as *Bulbophyllum*, the pseudobulbs are strung out along a horizontal stem and the one or two leaves arise from the apex of each pseudobulb. In some species the flower stem arises from the top of the pseudobulb and in others it appears at the base. The pseudobulb can be very hard and shining, almost like a large, green and unripe, very hard apple and be completely devoid of any ornamentation or covering, but occasionally it can be characteristically ribbed or otherwise marked and it is frequently densely clothed in either lining green leaves or dead and decaying brown leaf bases.

The size of pseudobulbs can vary enormously, the variation depending on both the species and the conditions under which the plants grow. A very good indication of the health of a greenhouse-grown orchid is the size of its pseudobulbs; if the plant has been properly cultivated, each succeeding pseudobulb will be at least as large as the preceding one. On the other hand, if the growing conditions are unsuitable and the plant has been starved or subjected to environmental extremes, the pseudobulbs get progressively smaller.

Although in each genus, or group of related genera, all the pseudobulbs are of the same general shape, with few exceptions the size is much more a specific feature. For example, nearly all of the 1,000 + species of the genus *Bulbophyllum* have ovoid or spheroid pseudobulbs, but they range in size from the mere pin-heads densely aggregated in the Australian *B. minutissimum* to the golf ball-sized ones of the evil-smelling carrion-flowered *B. fletcheranum* from New Guinea. The largest pseudobulbs are the 2–3½ metre (6½–11 ft) long cigar-shaped ones of *Grammatophyllum speciosum* from Malaysia and Indonesia.

Pseudobulbs are normally on or above the soil surface but the mosses and other plants on the branches of the trees on which they grow often conceal their bases. Nevertheless, they are quite definitely

Despite their appearance, the swollen stems typical of epiphytic orchids do not have the structure of true bulbs. These pseudobulbs often provide useful clues for identification. Those of the Central American Schomburgkia tibicinis *are hollow and often inhabitated by ants.*

classified as aerial parts of the plant and usually, being green, they manufacture food as well as storing it. In the terrestrial species, both those from the tropics and those from the cooler temperate regions, food storage is often in underground organs called tubers. During the unfavourable resting period, which is usually the winter in cooler areas and the summer in hotter regions, the orchids can lose their leaves and other aerial parts and perennate from season to season by means of these tubers. Sometimes the plants disappear completely below ground, but in certain species, such as many of the lady's tresses (*Spiranthes* species) and in the insect-imitating *Ophrys*, a few flattened leaves remain above ground, often as a rosette closely adpressed to the soil, just to keep the plant's metabolism in operation.

To the medieval herbalists and right back to the early Greeks the paired tubers of many European orchids were a source of wonderment, possibly because of their rather fancifully testiculate appearance but probably because of their reputation as the source of the supposedly very highly nutritious substance variously called 'salep', 'saloop', 'salop', or 'sahlep'. This substance, which by twentieth-century chemical analyses has been proved to be mainly non-nutritious mucilage with very small amounts of minerals and carbohydrates, was extracted from the tubers. In the early part of the nineteenth-century, London, as well as other cities in Europe, boasted of its large number of Salopian shops where salep was sold as a drink. One ounce was supposed to be able to sustain a labourer for a day and an infusion of salep with a slice of bread and butter was proclaimed a perfect breakfast for a chimney-sweep. The popularity of salep probably owed something to its reputation as a mild aphrodisiac, a reputation gained from the testiculate tubers from which it was extracted.

Leaves

Most species of orchids bear green leaves but the saprophytic ones, that is those that obtain their food supplies mainly from the dead and decaying remains of other plants, are usually devoid of green chlorophyll and their leaves can be a bright magenta pink, dull dingy brownish-purple or so pale buff as to be almost transparent. The leaves of many of these saprophytes are reduced in size, often giving the plant the appearance of being completely leafless.

Orchid leaves are very rarely hairy, almost never have serrated or otherwise ornamental edges, and are very little divided, but nevertheless there are many very distinctive leaves and leaf-arrangements in the orchid family. The usual leaf forms are strap- or tongue-shaped or oval-elliptical, with nearly every shape in between, and the sizes and proportions vary enormously. Some orchid leaves are almost circular in outline and others are awl-shaped, often with a channel along one side; some are boldly erect, whereas in many epiphytic species they droop down almost as if the plant were dying. The various ways in which the apex of the leaf of certain orchids is divided is almost a study in its own right. If an orchid has a divided leaf-apex, it is usually unequally lobed and the variations result from the differences in size and shape of the two unequal parts.

Orchid leaves can spring from the base of the plant or pseudobulb, from the apex of the pseudobulb, or they can be arranged at intervals along the stems. In some species the leaves are arranged in two apparently intricately interlocked parallel rows but in others the sequence along the stem can be leaf, root, flower, leaf, root, leaf and so on.

Leaf colours can be bright grass-green or deep blue conifer-green or anything in between, and in species of tropical lady's slippers the leaves are tessellated in two tones of green. Young leaves and those subjected to excessive light levels are often tinged with red or purple and some species retain a reddish-purple colouration in all parts throughout their life-cycle.

Flowers (Inflorescences)

It is the flowers that give orchids their very distinctive botanical nature and their marked human appeal. The flowers can be borne singly at the top of a stem or they can be borne as an inflorescence arising either at the top of the stem, or laterally or both laterally and apically. The inflorescence can be loosely arranged along the stem but in some species the individual flowers are tightly packed into a globose structure and surrounded by the gelatinous remains of the outer floral layer.

The more common florist's orchids give only a hint of the extraordinary range of flower shape, colour and size among species and hybrids.

Dendrochilum latifolium, an epiphytic species from the Philippines, shows very well a characteristic arrangement of flowers on the stem.

The structure of all orchid flowers is very similar, which is surprising for such a large family. Basically there are three sepals and three petals and the sexual organs are in the centre of these two whorls.

Sepals The sepals are often similar if not identical in colour, size and shape, but sometimes the middle or dorsal sepal is larger and somewhat differently shaped. The outer surface of the sepals can be different from the inner surface both in colour and ornamentation such as a ridge or crest.

Petals Orchid flower petals, or at least the two lateral ones, are frequently very similar to the sepals but the middle or dorsal petal of orchids is always very distinct from the three sepals and from the other two petals. It is this middle petal, always called the labellum or lip in orchids, which gives orchid flowers their characteristic appearance.

Labellum The labellum can be bigger than all the other flower parts put together or it can be very much smaller, but nearly always it is of a different size. The shape is also very distinctive and is one of the major botanical features used for distinguishing species within a genus. Labella can be entire, two-lobed, three-lobed or four- or more lobed, and this sub-division can be so extreme that the labellum resembles the nest-like strands of a lichen. The four-lobed labellum of some European species has the appearance of a human being or a monkey or other animal, and ever since the Middle Ages man has endowed the man orchid, lady orchid, military orchid, monkey orchid and lizard orchid with supernatural powers on account of the remarkable resemblance of their flowers to these creatures.

Another distinctive feature of the labellum is that its surface can be decorated with several kinds of outgrowth, usually a single ridged crest but occasionally a row of cushion-like hairs or calluses or overlapping plates. The inner surface of the labellum is often very hairy but in the case of the pitcher or bucket orchids the container-like labellum has an extremely smooth and shining slippery surface. The margin of the labellum is often frilled and ruffed, especially in highly bred 'horticultural plants'.

The labellum is frequently elongated backwards to form a spur, which can vary from a long dangling tube up to 35cm (14in) long to the merest sac-like swelling. In *Dendrobium* and some other genera the back of the labellum and the bases of the sepals and petals are joined together to form a spur-like chin called, technically, a mentum. Spurs and menta are occasionally bilobed or cleft. They are associated with pollinating mechanisms and usually contain some nectar at their bases, the pollinating insect usually having a proboscis just as long as the spur. The labellum is an attractive device for pollinating insects and acts as a landing platform for them.

Colours Orchid flowers vary in colour from purest whites, rich creams, yellows and greens through browns, reds, magenta, lilac, carmine and a range of pinks, to enamel blues and dullest rusty maroons and purples. In some species all floral parts are the same colour, in many others the sepals are quite distinctly coloured from the petals, but in the majority of

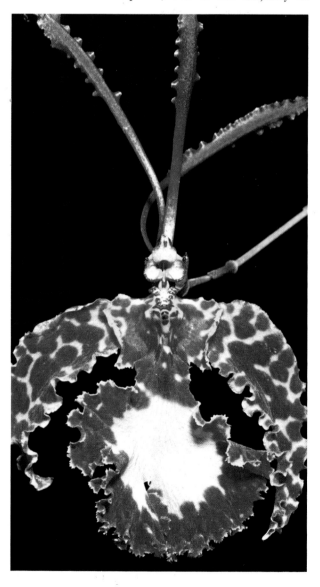

Even within a genus there can be great variety in the colour and shape of flowers. The genus Oncidium *consists of over 500 species, including flowers of very varied appearance. O.* krameranum *is one of the most insect-like of all orchids. This American species is often cultivated and has been used in breeding.*

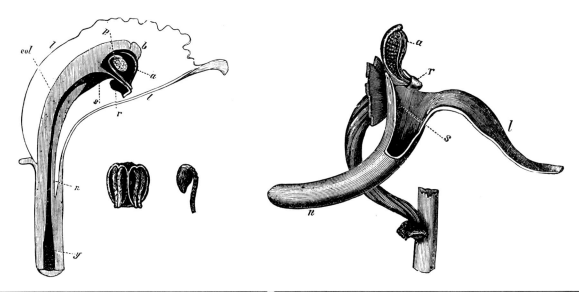

Top left : a cross-section of a Cattleya *flower (petals and sepals removed) showing detailed structure of the column, which consists of stamens and styles fused together ; a. anther, b. column-apex, p. pollinium, r. rostellum, s. stigmatic surface, col. column, l. labellum, n. nectary, y. ovary.*

Top right : side-view of Orchis mascula *flower (petals and sepals removed, labellum and part of the spur partially removed) ; a. anther, r. rostellum, s. stigma l. labellum, n. spur.*

Bottom : the green-flowered Cymbidium lowianum *is one of the most vigorous of* Cymbidium *species and was one of the parents of the first ever* Cymbidium *hybrid, C. Eburneo-lowianum.*

Opposite: the tropical Central American species Masdevallia erythrochaete *is often grown for its bizarre appearance.*

Above: Brassia longissima *is one of the longest sepalled of the fifty or so* Brassia *species, which are characterized by their tail-like sepals. The genus is closely related to* Oncidium, *with which it has recently been crossed to produce* Brassidium *hybrids.*

species it is the labellum that is quite different from the rest of the flower. The bizarre and unusual shapes of labella combined with their distinct colours are the features that makes orchids so different from all other plants. Labellum colour can be basically the same as the tepals (i.e. sepals plus petals), but this base colour is then variously spotted, blotched, streaked, veined or margined with a distinct hue. In many species, however, the labellum is quite distinct in colour and its spots, blotches and streaks, etc. are then even more strikingly different. Spots and blotches and so on are not only found on the labellum but the sepals and lateral petals are frequently ornamented, and in many species the entire flower presents an extraordinary appearance, with all parts heavily spotted.

The subtly complementary or bizarrely contrasting colours of the parts of orchid flowers are all part of the pollinating mechanism designed to attract the pollinating agents.

Scents As well as the oddly shaped flowers, orchids produce many scents, all probably further serving to entice pollinating insects. The scents range from sickly sweet overpoweringly cocoa-like perfumes, through purest lemons and orange-blossom to disgustingly pervasive putrifying flesh smells. These carrion-scented flowers are pollinated by flies that normally visit decaying flesh in order to deposit the eggs from which their maggots arise; in the case of the orchids, they transfer pollen from one flower to another.

Attracting pollinating insects by mimicry is characteristic of Caladenia *species (left) from Australia and* Ophrys *species (right) from Europe.*

The bizarre shapes and markings of the European Ophrys *orchids have given rise to many descriptive common names – for example, bee orchid, fly orchid and spider orchid. O.* cretica *is a fairly widely distributed Grecian and Cretan species.*

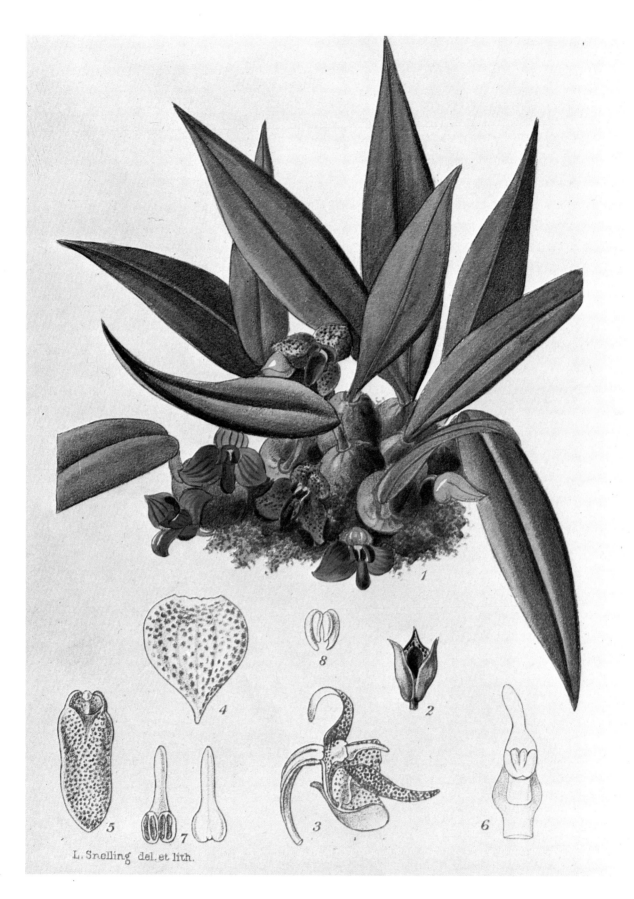

L. Snelling del. et lith.

Reproductive organs It is likely that most of the variations in the sizes, shapes, colours, scents and arrangement of orchid flowers have arisen over the ages in order that the right insect is available at the right time to be attracted to the flower to pollinate it. The word 'insect' is not quite exact as certain orchids have been recorded as being visited by hummingbirds, bats, frogs and snails, and these visits presumably effect a pollination. Sometimes it is a combination of all floral features that serves as the attractive device, as in the bee orchid's allies (*Ophrys* species) from Europe and in the Australian and South-East Asian genus *Cryptostylis*, where the flower resembles an insect's body. Male insects are attracted to the flower by its colour, size, scent, orientation and shape and attempt to mate with it. Their non-productive copulatory movements effect pollination: this mechanism is called 'pseudocopulation'.

In contrast to the other parts of the flower the sexual organs of orchids are quite simple at first glance. The sexual organs of orchids are always united into a single structure, called the column, lying opposite the labellum. In its simplest form, and it is very simple in most orchids, the column is literally like a column surmounted by the male anthers with a receptive female stigmatic surface underneath it which is usually separated from the anthers by a flap of non-reproductive tissue called the rostellum. It is the exact disposition and structure of the anthers, the stigma and the intervening rostellum that provides the technical basis for the classification of the orchid family.

The anther of orchids is a most unusual organ in that the pollen grains are not just a loose powder but are aggregated into two, four, six or eight mealy, horny or waxy pollen masses, technically called pollinia (singular: pollinium). These pollinia are usually covered by a hinged cap (anther cap) and are variously attached to the column apex and normally stalked.

Below the stigma is the ovary which, when fertilized, forms the seed capsule. When ripe, the capsule is usually brown and varies in shape from globular to a long thin tube-like structure. It sheds the minute dust-like seeds through longitudinal slits.

To be reliable, the pollinating mechanisms all depend on three factors. First they must attract the pollinating agent; second, they must ensure that this agent obtains the pollinia; and third, the agent must transfer the pollinia to the receptive stigmatic surface of another flower, preferably another flower on another plant to ensure cross-pollination. The attachment of the pollinia to the pollinator is facilitated by additional devices such as quick-drying glue or an explosive mechanism. Some orchid species are habitually self-pollinated but cross-pollination is the normal pattern and this cross-pollination frequently extends beyond the confines of the particular species to produce many natural hybrids. This promiscuity can extend to the production of hybrids between two species in different genera and, under the controlled experimentation of the orchid breeder, up to twenty species and five genera can be combined into one plant.

Classification

Despite the many attempts made in orchid periodicals and by the authoritative International Orchid Commission, very much confusion still exists in orchid growers' minds on many aspects of the classification and identification of orchids. This section of the book I hope will help clarify the situation.

Firstly, some definitions are necessary as confusion also exists in many people's vocabulary as to the meaning of such terms as classification and identification.

Taxonomy

This is the science of the classification of any objects, including living organisms, such as orchid plants, into a convenient system or class in order that they can be physically and mentally 'pigeon-holed', so that we may know a certain amount about their relationships to each other, and so that the objects classified bear a convenient and generally accepted label by which we may refer to them. As a generalization, the taxonomy or classification of orchids consists of placing essentially similar plants together and separating dissimilar plants. Thus we are all taxonomists when we mentally place two more or less identical plants

Trias picta *is a South-East Asiatic orchid, related to the very large genus* Bulbophyllum. *This plant is rarely seen in cultivation; this illustration from* Curtis's Botanical Magazine *(published since 1787 and prepared at the Royal Botanic Gardens, Kew, since 1841) is from a specimen flowering at Kew about fifty years ago. The illustration includes details of the flower base showing lateral sepals (2), the dorsal sepal (4), the labellum (5), the column (6), the pollinia (7), and the pollinia and stipes (8).*

25

together; the professional taxonomist's major task is to decide the degree of similarity and dissimilarity, and here lies the root of much of the confusion that exists in people's minds. The problem is that each taxonomist is entitled to his own opinions as to the relative importance of the type and character of each feature or group of features used in deciding on the limits of any classificatory group. There can be as many opinions, all equally valid but most misguided, as there are taxonomists and taxonomists themselves can change their minds! Mature consideration based on fuller and more detailed study of a greater and more comprehensive range of specimens leads most taxonomists to modify their opinions. In the early days of the taxonomy of orchids only a minute fraction of the world's orchid flora was known to man and this is why nearly all orchids were either placed in *Orchis* or *Satyrium* or *Ophrys* or *Epidendrum*. Linnaeus, in 1753, recognized about 70 species of orchid but today's cataloguing gives a minimum total of 18,000 species. A classification scheme devised for 70 plants is not valid for more than 250 times that number, although it must be stressed that the work of Linnaeus has laid the foundation for the taxonomic study of all plants.

Today, the taxonomist has at his command many sophisticated techniques which pinpoint differences between plants that could never have been seen just a few years ago. The chromosomes of an orchid cell, the ultra-structure of the pollen grains and the detailed chemical structure of orchid extracts are three examples of recently used taxonomic factors.

It must be emphasized that in this book the taxonomic information given, which really means the names of the plants, represents an opinion held by the author and is not, in any sense of the word, legally binding. However, the opinions I have expressed are those I feel would be a consensus of those held by a majority of practising botanists at the time of writing.

Systematics

Although systematics, classification and taxonomy are loosely interchangeable terms, systematics is more strictly the study of the arrangement of taxonomic groups into a hierarchial system in order to express more fully degrees of relationship. In the orchid family there have been many systematic classifications proposed and such is the nature of living organisms, especially in such a large and diverse group as the orchids, there can never be said to be a perfect classification.

However, the botanist attempts, in a systematic classification, to reflect the supposed evolution and development of the plants and those derived from common ancestors are grouped closer to each other than those from a more distant origin.

To start at the very beginning, a basic unit of classification is the *individual* plant. In nature, individual plants grow together and the resulting group is termed a *population*. When a taxonomist is considering a plant, he is automatically treating it as a representative sample of a population. Because of the dispersal of seeds and other propagules, most orchids, except the very rarest, exist in many, perhaps thousands of populations. All similar populations are grouped into the basic unit which is the *species*. There may be variations within a species, minor colour or shape variations are usually called *varieties* or *forms*; more significant variations, often with a geographical or habitat preference, are called *subspecies*. The systematist groups similar species together as a *genus* and in the orchid family the 18,000 species have been grouped into about 750 genera. In each genus there can be just a single species but many genera are much larger, such as the Asiatic *Dendrobium* with 1,400 species and the tropical American *Pleurothallis*, which had 1,000 species at the last assessment. There are many intermediate groupings between the genus and the family itself but in orchids the systematic botanist groups the 750 genera into about eighty *subtribes*, which, in turn, are distributed into six *tribes*, which, in turn, are aggregated into three *subfamilies* which together constitute the orchid *family*.

Nomenclature

The orchid grower only needs to be familiar with the *individual*, the *variety*, the *species*, the *genus* and the *subtribe*, and to enable him to do this he must learn to recognize the form of the words used for these categories. There is no commonly accepted term for

Ophrys argolica *is another of the small-flowered but curiously shaped and marked European orchids.*

the individual, and the genus, species and variety, although always Latinized and obeying the rules of the Latin language, have no well-defined and consistent structure. Examples of species names are *Paphiopedilum haynaldianum* or *Schwartzkopffia lastii*, and examples of varieties are *Habenaria gabonensis* var. *psiloceras* or *Dendrobium speciosum* var. *hillii*. However, the categories above this are much more regular with the *subtribe* ending in *inae* (e.g. *Lycastiinae*), the *tribe* in *eae* (e.g. *Vandeae*), the subfamily in *oideae* (e.g. *Cypripedioideae*) and the family itself in *aceae* (i.e. *Orchidaceae*).

This giving of names to these classificatory groups is called Nomenclature and is governed by a set of internationally accepted Rules called the *International Code of Botanical Nomenclature*. Taxonomically there can be as many opinions about a plant's position in a classificatory scheme as there are holders of opinions, but for each opinion there can be only one correct name. For the reader interested in the subject of nomenclature the International Code can be consulted but because of the special needs of the raisers and registrants of orchid hybrids the International Orchid Commission has produced a *Handbook on Orchid Nomenclature and Registration*, which deals not only with naturally occurring plants but also with the very intricate subject of the nomenclature of man-made hybrids (called *grexes*) and their varieties (called *cultivars*). Examples of these latter are *Odontoglossum* Opheon 'Majestic' where Opheon is the *grex* name and 'Majestic' is the *cultivar* name. Cultivar names are always enclosed in single quotes, e.g. 'Westonbirt', and although, like grex names, they are not usually in Latin form, they are nevertheless bound by the rules of orchid nomenclature. The *Handbook* referred to above gives details of the rules for the formation and application of grex and cultivar names and deals with the intricacies of *hybrid generic* names such as *Aëridocentrum* (i.e. *Aërides* × *Ascocentrum*) and *Hagerara* (i.e. *Doritis* × *Phalaenopsis* × *Vanda*).

Appendix A provides a useful list of all hybrid genera currently accepted.

Identification
Identification is the process of deciding to which species or variety or grex or cultivar a given plant should be assigned. Botanists at the great botanical institutes, like Britain's Royal Botanic Gardens at Kew, the British Museum (Natural History) in Kensington, or Bailey Hortorium in Ithaca, N.Y., spend much time identifying plants sent in by growers, collectors and explorers. For many parts of the world the orchid flora has been studied and the technical accounts of these floras, together with various 'keys' for identification, constitute the *Flora* of the country. Some botanists concentrate not on the flora of a particular region, but on all the species in a particular genus. The results of these studies are published as a *Monograph* and these monographs usually also contain identification keys.

Ecology

The orchid family is represented by one or more species in nearly every country of the world except the more isolated islands and in Antarctica, where there is little variety of any living organisms. However, orchids are found in such inhospitable places as Greenland and Iceland, and even in the desert countries such as many of those of North Africa, orchids thrive along the banks of water courses and in the wadis. The orchid floras of countries are very variable in diversity and the general rule is that the hotter and wetter tropical countries are very much richer than the drier ones. For example, Iraq has about twenty species whereas Papua New Guinea probably has at least 3,000 species, many of them yet undescribed and barely known to science.

Ecological range
This extensive geographical range of orchids is matched by their equally catholic ecological range. Although each species of orchid is usually only able to tolerate a limited range of habitats, the family as a whole has representatives in all the major vegetation types except those in the most extreme environments. Orchids are found in nearly every situation but the hottest and driest sandy deserts, the highest mountain summits, and the industrially despoiled lowlands and intensively agricultural regions.

In the hybrid Cymbidium King Arthur 'West of England', King Arthur is the grex name and 'West of England' the cultivar name.

This hybrid was first raised in 1963 in California, its parents being Cym. Sweetheart *and* Cym. Nila.

The tolerance of an orchid species to the environmental factors of soil type and nutrient and acidity levels, day length and light quality and intensity, water supply and nature, air currents and humidity, temperatures and competition with other plants and pressures from animals, depends mainly on the inherent nature of that particular species, but orchids are surprisingly adaptable and tolerant of quite extreme conditions. They have a reputation for being very difficult to grow and an alleged need for pampering if they are to flower in cultivation. This is not strictly true, as many orchids can be successfully transplanted into the alien and often unpredictable geographical and ecological conditions of a greenhouse. Nevertheless, many orchids are very sensitive to certain environmental pressures, especially atmospheric pollution and habitat disturbance, and this is why there is widespread concern for the continuing existence of many thousands of the already rare species of the tropics and sub-tropical regions.

We have no evidence as to the nature of the orchids that grew before man first appeared as they are too soft in texture to provide fossils. Today we have a great range of species exhibiting a great range of vegetative and floral form and we deduce that orchids have been evolving for a very long time, especially when we consider some of the extreme types found.

Saprophytes

In Australia there are two species, called *Cryptanthemis slateri* and *Rhizanthella gardneri*, that grow completely underground and never even approach the surface to flower. They obtain their food by saprophytism and not by photosynthesis from sunlight, air and water as do most green plants. Many orchids are saprophytic and obtain their nutriment from dead and decaying vegetable matter, but certain species have two morphologically similar forms, one of which is normal and green and the other devoid of chlorophyll and hence saprophytic. Saprophytic orchids are often very rapid growers as they are not dependent on light and in the tropics some saprophytic climbing orchids are reputed to grow at least 15 cm (6 in) each day. The Asiatic saprophyte *Galeola altissima* can have climbing stems up to 46 m (150 ft) long! Saprophytes are scattered throughout the orchid family and most countries have

The great majority of tropical orchids are epiphytic. Trichocentrum tigrinum, *from Ecuador, is remarkable in having minute pseudobulbs and in being capable of flowering when* *very small. It has been crossed with* Oncidium papilio *to give* Trichocidium Gold (1959).

at least one such plant in their floras. In Europe, the bird's nest orchid (*Neottia nidus-avis*) and the coral-root (*Corallorhiza trifida*) are saprophytes; in North America *Hexalectris* species are quite common in the south-east and the ten species of native *Corallorhiza* between them cover the whole country; in tropical Africa the species of several genera are entirely saprophytic. *Epipogium*, *Didymoplexis* and *Auxopus* are examples, and there are too many examples to enumerate in the rich floras of the tropical jungles of South America and South-East Asia.

Many saprophytes are leafless but this peculiarity is not only found in this group. In plants of such genera as *Microcoelia* from Africa and *Taeniophyllum* from Asia the general appearance is of a mass of roots surmounted by a very insignificant flower spike. These roots are quite substantial and green and have taken over the usual photosynthetic activity of the leaves. It has been shown that the colouring matter of some green-flowered orchids is a chlorophyll-like substance and that the flowers, as well as having the normal reproductive function, also provide the food!

Epiphytes

Mention has already been made of the two groups into which orchids can be divided: the epiphytes and terrestrials. The presence of saprophytism in both of these groups gives four major orchid types but there are many further subdivisions. For example, many epiphytes grow on rocks as well as on the bark of trees and some are confined exclusively to rock-surfaces, where they grow among a mat of mosses and lichens: these rock growers are strictly lithophytes.

Aquatic orchids

There are no truly aquatic orchids but habitats where the water level is at or just above or below the soil level, such as marshes, fens, bogs and swamps, are often very rich in orchid species. The North American 'nodding lady's tresses' (*Spiranthes cernua*) grows in marshy fields and meadows, wet woods and in shallow streams and lakesides, and can be completely covered for part of the year when growing in roadside ditches.

Similarly, although there are no strictly marine species, there are many species that can tolerate a salty atmosphere. In Britain, for example, the cliffs

and cliff-tops are a favourite site for orchid hunters, and in the tropics the coastal tree belt and mangrove forests are often festooned with orchids.

Woodland species

It is the woodlands and forests of the all climatic zones of the world that provide a home for the majority of orchids. Some plants, such as the European *Dactylorhiza fuchsii*, are found in open grassland and in fairly dense woodland, but usually woodland species are tolerant of only a small light range. The more constant humidity of a forest also controls their spread. It is too cold in the winter or too dry in the summer for orchids to grow as epiphytes in the woodlands of the temperate and Mediterranean type climates, but in the tropics epiphytes are a major feature of forest trees. Tropical rain forests in the wide equatorial belt across South America, Africa, Asia and into north Queensland and the Pacific islands hold about half of the world's orchid species and the great majority of these are epiphytes. The tall and many-layered tree-canopy with its thick layer of climbers and epiphytes, consists not only of orchids but ferns, figs, bromeliads and mosses, and casts such a dense shade that forest-floor species are comparatively infrequent. However, where they do occur, they can form a continuous cover of a single species. There is a group of orchids called the 'Jewel' orchids because of their silvery veined velvet-sheened deep green and maroon leaves and it is often these species that form the ground cover. Jewel orchids are unique among cultivated orchids in that they are grown for their leaves, the flowers in many cases being insignificant, often grotesquely twisted and of a dingy stained white colour.

Where there is more light, such as at the forest margin or along trackways and where trees have been felled or have fallen down, terrestrial orchids are quite common. Many of our European rarities are found in such situations.

Wetland orchids

Another very popular habitat for terrestrial species is in marshes, bogs and wet meadows, where the acidity of the water and the amounts of nutrients available determine the particular species that will thrive

The Brazilian species Cattleya intermedia *is often used in breeding programmes. As well as growing truly epiphytically on trees this* Cattleya *also grows epilithically.*

there. By virtue of their size and flower colour the orchids in these situations are usually the most conspicuous plants. Occasionally they all belong to one species but frequently several related species grow together and swarms of hybrid plants, showing a great range of characters, are often found.

Unfortunately, orchids of the wet habitats, such as marshes, are becoming increasingly scarce because of the drainage which is carried out to provide more land for agriculture and housing and industrial use. Orchids are sensitive to the presence of certain pollutive substances in ground-water and these are becoming quite common even in very rural areas.

Grassland orchids

Ploughing, liming, fertilizing or excessive grazing have had a detrimental effect on the numbers and variety of orchids growing in fields and arable lands. Before the Second World War orchids were common in fields and downland throughout England but the increased demand for food led to the ploughing-up of these very ancient pastures and species such as the green-winged meadow orchid (*Orchis morio*), pyramidal orchid (*Anacamptis pyramidalis*) and the burnt orchid (*Orchis ustulata*) are now very rare. However, there are still large areas of lightly grazed chalk and limestone grassland in all parts of Europe and in May and June, and July in the northern parts, they can be ablaze with orchid flowers.

Savannah orchids

In the tropics and sub-tropics, the savannahs (which are basically rough scrubby grasslands interspersed with scattered groups of trees) can carry a varied orchid flora with both terrestrials and epiphytes. From earliest times savannahs in long-inhabited countries have been subjected to periodic fires but the orchids have adapted to survive this environmental shock and in some cases only flower after a fire. Examples include the South-African yellow-flowered *Penthea patens* from the south-western Cape Province and *Pachites bodkinii*, which is more widespread.

Orchids as weeds

It is surprising that orchids, with their wide ecological range, are not found more often as weeds of disturbed and cultivated ground. Out of the 18,000 or more species presently accepted less than ten could be classified as weeds, but many species have been introduced from one country to another and are to-day considered as fully naturalized. The best-known examples include the now widespread American *Epidendrum radicans* and the Asiatic trio of *Arundina bambusifolia*, *Phaius tancarvilliae* and *Spathoglottis plicata*. *Zeuxine strateumatica* from Asia has become naturalized in Florida and the common British species *Dactylorhiza maculata*, *Epipactis helleborine* and *Listera ovata* are now well-established in the United States and Canada.

In greenhouses where orchids are grown the widespread Asiatic ladies'-tresses, *Spiranthes sinensis*, and the Madagascan *Cynorkis fastigiata* can very nearly be considered as greenhouse weeds.

Orchids and animals

Ecology deals with the home life of organisms and an account of orchid ecology must not neglect to mention the animals with which they are associated. All animals require plants as these are the sole source of food, but not all plants require animals except as constituents of the soil maintaining its fertility characteristics. Animals, usually insects and most often bees, wasps, flies and butterflies and moths, are frequently the pollinating agents of plants and also assist in the dispersal of ripe seeds. In orchids, the pollinating agents include not only representatives of almost every group of insects but also humming-birds and honey-eaters, snails, frogs and bats. The seeds of orchids are usually wind-dispersed.

History

It was the Ancient Greeks who originated the word 'orchid', which comes from their word 'orchis', testicle. Dioscorides believed that orchids had magic aphrodisiacal properties and, if eaten by the father or mother, could determine the sex of an unborn child. As the Greek civilization declined, their knowledge of plants was passed to the rest of Europe, and the ideas of the medieval herbalists were very obviously derived from those of the Greeks. The relationship between

The early marsh orchid, Dactylorhiza incarnata, *is widespread in damp areas all over the British Isles and Europe.*

orchids and sex was still very evident; for example, it was thought that many of the European wild orchids arose in the fields by fermentation of the damp soil with spermatic fluid spilled by copulating domestic animals. Certainly the animal-like appearance of the flowers of the bee- (*Ophrys apifera*), wasp- (*Ophrys apifera var. trollii*), fly- (*Ophrys muscifera*), lizard- (*Himantoglossum hircinum*), spider- (*Ophrys fuciflora* and *O. sphegodes*) and monkey-orchid (*Orchis simia*) must have had an effect on the average uneducated person and even today the native orchids of temperate climates are as bizarre as any tropical plants.

Shakespeare refers to orchids only in *Hamlet*, where

'long purples', 'dead men's fingers' and the shepherds' 'grosser name', all probably references to the early purple orchid (*Orchis mascula*), are mentioned.

We know relatively little of the domestic life of the eastern countries, such as China and Japan, during the early years of their civilization, but we know that many orchids grew in those countries and that they cultivated many plants in their homes. Almost certainly orchids were taken into cultivation by the Chinese and Japanese but the evidence we do have is that orchids were grown for the beauty of their leaves

as well as that of the flowers. Cymbidiums, which today are possibly the most widely cultivated group of orchids, were grown by these eastern countries. Not only were they natives and therefore easily available, they are also easy to grow and the flowers are often very long-lived.

There is no definite indication that the spectacular early American civilizations especially revered orchids, although the Spanish conquerors recorded that such plants as *Cattleya citrina* were known to the natives and possibly worshipped by them.

The exploration of the Indian sub-continent by the English and the East Indies by the Dutch, both peoples having a deep-rooted interest in natural history, led to many orchids being recorded, illustrated and collected. Many of the surviving drawings are surprisingly true to life and were drawn not by Europeans but by natives of the countries in which the plants grew.

Much of this information on tropical orchids was published in various accounts of the time, but of greatest importance to botanists and zoologists is the magnificent compilation carried out by the 'Complete Naturalist', the Swedish Carl von Linné (or Linnaeus as he is usually called). In Linnaeus' *Species Plantarum* published in 1753, all the species known to date were recorded. The taxonomy and nomenclature of orchids, and of all flowering plants, date from 1753, and it is surprising how accurately Linnaeus described many of the species in his volumes.

It is known that attempts were made to import living orchids into the horticulturally-aware countries such as England, Belgium, France and Holland at this time, but success in growing and flowering these plants was very limited.

The first tropical orchid to flower in Europe was a supposedly dried, preserved specimen of *Bletia verecunda* which was sent from the Bahamas to Peter Collinson in England. As it showed some signs of life he sent it to his friend Sir Charles Wager, who planted it in his warm greenhouse, where it flowered the following summer. This was in 1733 and since that date probably half of the known total species of orchid, currently estimated at 18,000, have been brought to Europe in attempts to cultivate them. A great proportion of these came to Britain and even today, if a

A somewhat fanciful depiction of an Orchis *or* Ophrys *from John Gerard's* Herball *(1597). This was the most popular and influential English herbal in spite of, or perhaps because of, its mixture of close observation and credulous fantasy.*

catalogue was made of all the species present in Britain in the living state, it would probably number about 6,000. Ever since those far-off days when the first specimen flowered, orchids have been regarded in Britain as a prerogative of the rich, and they were considered at one time the ultimate symbol of wealth and success in life.

The very fact that it proved so difficult successfully to grow and even keep alive the first importations, let alone flower them, contributed towards this aura of richness and luxury that surrounds orchids. The early English growers kept their orchids always in very hot and steamy 'stove' houses, believing, as do so many people today, that orchids are always from incredibly warm and humid tropical jungle habitats. In these incorrect conditions many plants died, but, instead of the would-be orchid growers giving up trying to culti-

The interior of a 'stove' house dating from about 1860. Orchids were grown wherever there was room – on the floor, on benches and in hanging pots and baskets.

vate them, they were spurred on to greater efforts.

The early importations to Britain were from the West Indies because the trading connections with these countries were strongest at that time. The great continents of Asia and Africa had still to open up their treasure house of wonderful plants and flowers to European eyes. *Epidendrum rigidum*, *E. fragans*, *E. cochleatum*, and a *Vanilla* sp. were examples of early successful importations to Britain. Soon, however, a few plants found their way to English greenhouses from China and about 1780 *Phaius tancarvilliae* and *Cymbidium ensifolium* were recorded in flower in an amateur gardener's greenhouse in Yorkshire.

The pre-eminence of Britain in the field of natural history and horticulture, not so marked now as in the last century, has risen from the fact that the amateur and the professional, whether he be plant collector, grower or botanist, have always worked together, rarely competing but always collaborating. From 1790 onwards more and more occurrences of tropical orchids flowering in Britain are reported, from the collections of professional horticulturists, rich amateurs and scientifically run botanic gardens such as Kew and Oxford. The spread of the British Empire obviously contributed immensely towards the flow of plants to Britain; the colonial administrators and other colonists no doubt being overawed by the splendours of the tropical orchid floras they encountered sent plants to their friends and to botanical establishments at home. Botanical gardens

were also established in many parts of the Empire and the directors of these establishments were usually in contact with similar gardens or commercial nursery-men in England.

The more enterprising members of the aristocracy, or perhaps it was just the richer ones, were not content just to receive orchid plants in a rather haphazard way or to purchase them from commercial concerns, so they sent out their own collectors. Even before this the Royal Botanic Gardens at Kew had sent Francis Masson, a Scot, on an expedition to South Africa, to explore the botanical riches of the southern hemisphere.

It would be difficult to mention names of growers, explorers, and of their patrons and sponsors, because so many would be omitted. The exploits of Admiral Bligh and the botanical and horticultural achievements of Lobb, Wallich, Loddiges, Gibson, Roxburgh and Bateman, for example, have been written about many times.

As the latter half of the last century was starting, two important events in English orchid culture occurred which have governed the subsequent development of this branch of horticulture ever since. The large commercial establishments of orchid nurserymen in Britain and on the European mainland, firms such as Veitch, Low, Van Houtte and Linden, were challenged by a Prussian émigré, Frederick Sander, who, from very humble beginnings, set up the largest orchid nursery yet known. Such was his ability, both as a businessman and as an organizer of collectors and explorers, that he was known as the Orchid King. Mail addressed to him in this way, with no indication of place other than England, reached him without delay. The Russians created him a baron of the Holy Russian Empire, the crowned heads of Europe were his customers, and Queen Victoria appointed him Royal Orchid Grower. From that time commercial orchid growing, mainly to supply the collections of rich amateurs, became a very definite industry, possibly on the decline in Britain but decidedly still expanding in many English-speaking countries such as the United States, Australia and Singapore.

Sander imported vast quantities from many parts of the world: staff were employed day and night on many occasions at the private railway sidings at the nursery at St. Albans, unpacking fresh consignments which were sent immediately by express train after being unloaded at various points. A few people were concerned about the wanton destruction of large populations of species by commercial collectors at that time, but Victorian England was a long way from the jungles and sadly, even today, one still learns of

From about 1875, popular genera were cultivated on a large commercial scale. Odontoglossums have always been popular subjects, as in this Odontoglossum *house dating from about 1900, as they require relatively little heat and are profuse in their flowering.*

these veritable rapes, carried out by unscrupulous collectors to ensure the rarity of a particular orchid.

In those earlier times single plants were often sold for over a hundred guineas, and there are records of some reaching six hundred guineas each. The other event, probably of even greater significance than the rise of the large commercial orchid nurseries, was the flowering of the first orchid hybrid by the head gardener of Messrs. Veitch, Mr. John Dominy. This was *Calanthe masuca* × *C. furcata*, now called *C. Dominyi*. It was the forerunner of the vast orchid-

breeding industry, an industry in which the number of new hybrids raised is now increasing by about three a day, every day of the week, every week of the year, a rate maintained for the last twenty years and showing no sign at all of lessening.

The history of orchids is still being made. Expeditions sponsored by national scientific institutions still explore the tropical jungles of Asia, Africa and America and many new orchid species, never before described and often of decided horticultural value, are discovered. As these expeditions are primarily to collect specimens for study in the herbarium and laboratory, most orchids and other plants are preserved by pressing and drying or in an alcohol-water preserving fluid so that they can be sent back to Europe or North America with as many of their important characters as possible. Although preservation in these ways destroys the colour of the plants and their flowers, the great development of colour photography in the last twenty years has meant that expeditions return with as many rolls of exposed colour films as flattened dingy-brown specimens. Suitable plants of orchids are air-freighted back for cultivation, although the demands of conservation have now made this more selective.

To mention my own experiences in the British Solomon Islands Protectorate, when I was a member of the Royal Society's expedition in 1965, will give an idea of the orchid riches still to be discovered in a relatively small area. Six months of fairly concentrated orchid-hunting in the unexplored rain-forests and along the coastal mangrove swamps resulted in over a thousand collections of orchids being made. Most were preserved by the traditional method of pressing and drying but the complicated and essentially three-dimensional orchid flowers were preserved in preserving fluid, and nearly two hundred living plants were air-freighted back to the Royal Botanic Gardens at Kew.

Although the expedition was immeasurably better equipped and better organized than many of the earlier ones to the south Pacific, even the help of at least ten native porters and botanical assistants to each botanist did not prevent many specimens rotting before they could be preserved. Another hazard was the camp sites being flooded from nearby rivers, which would rise several feet in almost as many minutes. Despite these minor upsets, the subsequent study of the orchids collected revealed that the Islands, excluding Bougainville which now belongs to Papua New Guinea, had at least 250 different species of orchids, of which about one third are apparently confined to the area, one third also occur in neighbouring islands such as New Guinea and Fiji and the remainder are widespread throughout South-East Asia. Of the 250 species now known to occur there, only seventy had been recorded before the expedition.

The following are selected extracts from the

Above: James Veitch jr., the grandson of John Veitch, the founder of the famous orchid nursery firm, concerned himself mainly with the growing of orchids while John Gould Veitch travelled all over the old world collecting new species for the nursery.

Opposite: when the early plant collectors landed on tropical shores, they found the fringing coastal mangrove forests festooned with epiphytic orchids.

author's diary, recording some of the memorable episodes of the Royal Society's Expedition to the British Solomon Islands.

Friday, 23rd July

A perfect day with clear blue skies and hot sun with, however, a pleasant cooling slight breeze. I walked about one mile up the Pegato river which was now down to normal height and fordable at almost every point. The trees overhanging the river were festooned with orchids of several genera, not all flowering unfortunately:—*Coelogyne* (2 spp.), *Bulbophyllum* (6 spp.), *Dendrobium* (5 spp.), *Taeniophyllum* (a single plant with far larger flowers than one associates with the genus), *Liparis* (2 spp.), *Eria* (1 or 2 spp.), *Ceratostylis*, *Ephemerantha*, *Diplocaulobium*, *Appendicula* and two sarcanthoid genera. It was the richest day for orchids so far in the Solomon Islands, both for quantity and variety seen, and for the size and beauty of the flowers. The most spectacular was a single but absolutely perfect flower of *Coelogyne speciosa* with a large-flowered *Bulbophyllum* coming a close second. Another large-flowered *Coelogyne* with bright ginger-red markings was growing in some abundance. Probably the most attractive plant was the *Dendrobium* with tight clusters of pure white flowers relieved by the rose-pink apex of the labellum.

This was growing in festoons from a felled tree overhanging the river. A pure white-flowered *Begonia* was frequently seen in the deep shade cast by the overhanging trees. The rest of the land party soon arrived and set up camp but the evening was marred by heavy rain which continued more or less all night.

Sunday, 25th July

A bright rain-free morning, and I decided to go downstream to see if there was anything different at the confluence of the Warahito and the small stream about a quarter of a mile below the confluence of the Warahito and Pegato rivers. After crossing the Warahito a couple of times we had to cross it again for George Hemmen to film. It was almost chest high and very fast, but fortunately clear, so that one could see the bottom which, as in so many rivers here, is composed of a mixture of many types of rock, all worn into smooth pebbles. Where the small stream enters the Warahito a *Thrixspermum* was collected in full flower. Further up the stream three species of *Oberonia* were collected. Only two were in flower but I decided to collect the third species which was in fruit in the hope that it would be possible to match it vegetatively. The smaller-flowered *Coelogyne* was seen several times and growing with it were several robust fruiting specimens of *Pholidota*. About a quarter of a mile upstream a very peculiar *Bulbo-*

phyllum was growing on a tree overhanging the water. Instead of a long rhizome or creeping stem with pseudobulbs and leaves and flowering stems arising at more or less regular intervals, this species consisted of unconnected clumps of two to four pseudobulbs, each bearing a leaf and a deep crimson basal flower. Heavy but intermittent rain caused us to return to camp at about 15.30. At 16.30 the Warahito was still at normal height and quite clear but at 16.40 it rose about two feet in five minutes and was a very muddy colour. It took the Pegato river by surprise: the muddy Warahito water went *up* the still clear Pegato river, and for five minutes the water flow was reversed. There had probably been a very heavy rainfall higher up the Warahito valley to cause this sudden change. Ken Lee managed to get his radio to work and we heard that some places on the weather coast of Guadalcanal had just experienced 108 inches of rain in eight days. We bought some superb bananas, pink skinned and very large, from a native who had a large fruiting specimen of *Lycopodium* draped around his hat and on his banana-carrying stick. At first he tried to sell it to Tony Braithwaite but when we bought his bananas he handed it over free. It had not previously been seen by any of us on San Cristobal. It started to rain at 20.00 hours.

Tuesday, 31st August

Whitmore, Lee and Peake left for the lower camp. When we arrived yesterday they seemed very demoralized, saying that it was very wet here, very cold and very windy and very tough going up the slopes to the summit. We wished them luck among the mosquitoes and mud down below. Braithwaite and I left at 8.30 with Francis, Henry, Ruru, Tanasio and Seelua, to attempt to reach the summit. We were told that it would take $3\frac{1}{2}$ hours but we had high hopes as we started in bright sun and with a bright blue sky. The first 1,500ft was a fairly steep upward walk, not very muddy or mossy and quite warm. At about 4,200ft the slope suddenly increased and it was no longer possible to walk, but one had to scramble using hands and feet. At this point the moss layer suddenly became much thicker and all the trees became festooned with thick ginger and green cushions of mosses and liverworts. The tree roots were covered with moss and it was difficult to find a place to walk

without one's foot going into a soft mass of moss covering the roots. The only injuries I suffered were two bruises on my head gained by standing up too soon after crawling underneath the big roots. Bamboos were everywhere and provided very good drinking water, each internode containing about three tablespoonsful of cold, pleasant-tasting water. Suddenly the tree growth became more stunted, the trees became very shrubby and thickly branched and the mosses covered all the vegetation. However, the trees were more openly spaced and on looking at the altimeter, I found we were at 5,450ft. The last fifty feet were much flatter and suddenly I was at the summit. Tony Braithwaite had taken one hour and three-quarters and I took two and a quarter. Several orchids were growing on the moss at the summit but most of them were sterile. A *Mediocalcar* sp. was everywhere and an *Aglossorhyncha* sp. was on the moss on almost every tree trunk. Both these species had been flowering and had unripe capsules topped by the gelatinous mass of decaying flowers. A brilliant orange and a brilliant rosy-magenta *Dendrobium* sp. were in flower and also seen was a very sweetly scented *Phreatia*. Several small non-orchidaceous herbs were in flower including a blue-flowered *Burmannia*. On the rim of the crater we could just see the tops of trees and tree ferns but the bottom, 2,000ft down, was covered in cloud. Returning we collected until 4,000ft, when the rain forced us to return rapidly. It was really low cloud depositing its rain and this meant that the temperature dropped and we felt cold. For the first time since coming to the Solomon Islands, my feet felt cold!

Friday, 20th October

I felt better and, it being a warmer, clearer and dry morning, decided to walk up towards the summit. After about an hour's easy climbing through alternating zones of moss and bamboo forest the path levelled out, the trees became stunted and I was at the top of Mt. Popamanatseu. After all the days of preparation and planning and carrying and walking, to find the summit so easily accessible from the camp was rather an anticlimax. Another fifteen minutes' walk and I was on a similar but larger plateau at about the same height. With all the maps of the Solomon Islands there are serious discrepancies in the nomen-

The hot and humid tropical climate of the British Solomon Islands Protectorate makes an early start for orchid-collecting treks very necessary.

clature of the villages, rivers and mountains. All the small-scale maps show Mt. Popamanatseu as 8,oooft but the large-scale plans and maps show it as 7,oooft and also show an unnamed peak at 8,oooft. The altimeter showed we were at 7,oooft and, although it was a clear day, I could see no other peak higher than the one I was on, and furthermore, the ridges fell away in all directions. The summit vegetation was a thick carpet of mosses and liverworts with the damp hollows full of *Sphagnum* species. The 'herb' layer was mainly *Gleichenia vulcanica* and scattered *Lycopodium* species. The shrubs or really stunted trees were mainly *Myrtaceae* and all were thickly covered with moss around their swollen boles but their branches were more or less devoid of any growth except for a few clumps of a miniature *Dendrobium* with brilliant vermilion flowers. The mossy boles were the habitat of two orchids, both *Dendrobium* or *Glossorhyncha* types with many branched stems, woody and nearly always non-flowering. A couple of specimens of each were found eventually, one having a white and cream flower and the other a head of pure-white flowers relieved only by a rosy apex to the labellum. This was the same species as I had found on San Cristobal on the trees overhanging the Warahito river about one mile south of the Pegato-Warahito camp site. The most interesting find was a large-flowered *Dendrobium* of the *D. sophronites* and *D. cuthbertsonii* type, usually deep rosy-magenta in colour, but like the New Guinea plants varying in colour from palest rose to almost purple. The flowers varied in size to a certain extent. Other finds of orchid interest were a fine white-lipped *Calanthe* and a common terrestrial with dense spikes of white flowers with orange labellum, surrounded by whitish-green bracts. The proto-orchis found on Kalombangara occurs here in quantity and, very much like it in all respects except that they possess pollinia and a single leaf, a green- and a red-flowered species of *Liparis*. All in all a very satisfying day enhanced by the perfect weather which enabled me to take many photos from the summit. A considerable portion of Guadalcanal could be seen, the weather coast, Honiara, Mt. Gallego and beyond Ngela, even as far as Malaita and Santa Ysabel on the horizon.

Even today, plant collecting expeditions are at the mercy of the elements, as this flooded campsite in the British Solomon Islands Protectorate shows.

Where to Grow Orchids

The title of this chapter really refers to the cultivation of non-native species, as orchids native to one's country can usually be grown successfully in a garden provided the right conditions are given and that competition from other cultivated plants and weeds is controlled. In very large countries with a range of climates this generalization needs some qualification; for example, the sub-tropical species of Florida will not survive out of doors in the sub-zero temperatures experienced in the winter of some northern and central states of the United States of America.

Such is the perverse nature of modern man that the popular aphorism that 'the grass is always greener on the other side' applies very aptly to orchids. Native species are very rarely cultivated in any country, the most popular species being generally those which originate in distant and therefore more 'exotic' countries.

Despite the obvious beauty of many native species and their ease of cultivation, they are usually only considered worth growing by gardeners from other countries. This has led to a vast international exporting and importing trade in exotic orchids and an equally important one in providing the equipment for cultivating them.

Unless the climate is very similar in all respects to that of the plant's original home, a special shelter will be required for successful and continued cultivation. In all but the hottest countries this shelter will take the form of a greenhouse or lath-house depending on the degree of environmental control required. For the orchid grower with very little space, an indoor greenhouse or a 'picture window' will provide the right conditions for many orchids. It is not necessary to devote the greenhouse or other shelter entirely to orchids as the conditions provided may well be suit-able for other plants. Today there is an increasing tendency to grow other plants, such as ferns, bromeliads, begonias and epiphytic cacti, alongside orchids. Conversely, however, not all orchids can be grown in the same house, even if they all come from the same country. For example, in Borneo and New Guinea the orchids that grow in the very equitable environment of the coastal mangrove swamps require quite different conditions from those that grow in the jungle, and those from the dwarf moss-forests of the upper slopes of mountains require a distinctly cooler and more humid situation than those lower down.

In the early days of orchid growing the greenhouses were called after the generic names of the plants which grew in them and every orchid grower had, for example, a *Cattleya* house and a *Dendrobium* house. As more and more species became tested in cultivation, and more and more information became available about their growth requirements, the greenhouses became known as either cool, intermediate or warm, depending on the temperature regimes adopted. It is not essential to have three separate greenhouses to grow a great variety of orchids as most greenhouses can have partitions installed to produce two or three compartments with the conditions for each individually controlled. Even without partitions, it is possible to grow plants from a fairly wide range of habitats because each part of a greenhouse has its own microclimatic features and sunlight and ventilation can be regulated over a small area. A large plant can be used to provide a shadier and damper microclimate for a small plant. The degree of massing or spacing of plants can have a marked effect on the plants concerned, as each plant produces its own microclimate affecting itself and its neighbours.

If there is neither room for a greenhouse in the garden or attached to a wall of the house, nor the space

Phalaenopsis *Hollywood is a popular hybrid raised by the Robert Bean Nursery (San Fernando, California) in 1956. Its parents are* Phal. *Grace Palm and* Phal. *Thomas Tucker.*

available indoors for a 'Plantarium' or indoor 'mini'-greenhouse, nor the possibility of growing orchids on the windowsill or in a 'picture window', there is always the cellar to consider. It is unfortunate, in many ways, that many houses are no longer designed to include a cellar, and the lack of such a very useful plant-growing space is an important loss. Traditionally cellars were used for mushroom growing or for brewing, but with the minimum amount of conversion they can form ideal orchid houses. Temperatures are low but fluctuate very little in a cellar and therefore orchid-growing temperatures can be accurately controlled. As there is no ambient light, all light has to be provided by fluorescent tubes of the correct colour, temperature and intensity but modern control equipment is available to enable the orchid grower to control the conditions very accurately. There are several specialized books available on orchid growing under lights and these should be consulted.

Greenhouse construction

Orchids will grow in any type of greenhouse or even an indoor plantarium or picture window, provided there is some approximation to their natural requirements of moisture, food and temperature. Some orchids, such as very specialized saprophytes, will not survive any transplanting from the wild, but the great majority of orchids that are worth growing because of the appeal of their attractive or bizarre flowers can be cultivated and will survive.

However, for orchids to thrive rather than merely survive, considerable care has to be afforded them in details of temperature and humidity control and it is very much easier to provide this care if the greenhouse is of a suitable type. All greenhouses, whatever their pattern, can be made suitable for orchid growing, but it is always very much easier to start with the one that

gives the greatest flexibility so that whatever type of orchid is grown the greenhouse will suffice.

Orchid cultivation can require the grower to spend considerable periods in the greenhouse tending the plants and even when there is no 'tending' to be done, some time has to be spent enjoying the flowers of one's labours. Therefore, a basic requirement for an orchid house is that the ridge and the eaves must be sufficiently high to allow a comfortable working position. If too high, there will be too much air to heat and keep warm and a compromise must be arrived at. Most greenhouses on the market, whether they are steel, aluminium or wooden framed, are well-designed to cope with quite tall gardeners but not to waste space.

A basic requirement of a greenhouse for orchids is that the temperature range each day should not be too great and that in any case the temperature must not fall below a certain minimum depending on the type of plant grown. There is also a very important factor in orchid growing and that is that any temperature drop must be slow, as a sudden chill can cause bud-drop and otherwise damage a plant. A sliding door, through which the grower can squeeze, is much better than a normal hinged door which, when opened, allows a large proportion of the heated air to escape. If a porch or entrance hall, or a double-door acting as an airlock, can be incorporated, this is ideal.

In the early days of orchid growing, orchid houses were often half sunk into the ground so that from a distance they looked like a giant garden frame. These orchid 'pits', as they were called, had very low walls and the staging surface was usually at ground level, and the house was entered down some steps sunk into the ground. The advantage of these houses was that the earth around them and the relatively small amount of glass enabled an even temperature to be maintained. They were rarely used for growing those orchids that need a high temperature, such as Cattleyas and Vandas but those that prefer a damper and cooler regime, such as Paphiopedilums and Lycastes, reached their peak of perfection in these structures.

The advent of cheap plastic film, which enables a gardener very easily to double glaze a greenhouse to prevent excessive heat loss in winter, and also fan heaters, which spread warm air very quickly and thus prevent temperature gradients across a house, have meant that orchid pits are rarely built today. In any case their installation and maintenance costs are very much higher than those of conventional greenhouses.

The advice to all would-be orchid growers is to get as many catalogues as possible from greenhouse manufacturers and specialist agencies and study them for some time before deciding which will suit the needs of the plants, the space available in the garden and the size of the budget available. If possible, buy a greenhouse that can be extended so that it does not become necessary to get rid of surplus plants. With a series of extensions and partitions it is possible to grow orchids from a range of habitats.

Greenhouse equipment

Benching
Although many orchids can be grown in beds at ground level, it is usual for greenhouse orchids to be grown at waist-high staging or benching so that they can be easily tended and can obtain as much light as possible. The usual layout of a greenhouse consists of a central path with benching each side and usually at one end as well. The benching can be brick or concrete-block walling supporting a wooden framework or this can be supported on wooden legs. The

Opposite : a typical large orchid house is equipped with staging and is divided into sections for plants requiring different temperatures.

Above : tiered staging allows for an effective display and plants can be easily maintained.

use of aluminium and galvanized steel benching and supports is increasing in popularity but there are visual incongruities in growing plants in a glass and metal environment! Ideally the bench top should be covered with fairly coarse gravel in a plastic or rust-proof container, in which the base of the plant container can rest and which can be kept constantly damp to maintain both soil and atmospheric humidity. At least once a year the benching should be thoroughly cleaned to remove fungal and algal growth and any dead plant material and soil particles.

Watering Equipment

As many orchid collections belong to very busy people with relatively little time available for their hobby, and as very few amateur growers are able to afford a full-time paid gardener, it is essential that the orchid plants do not suffer from extremes of environmental conditions when their owner is not available. Orchid plants suffer from too little or too much water but by installing automatic watering equipment this problem can be largely obviated. There are many patented types of water device but basically they are of two main types. The more usual 'capillary' type is that in which the gravel or sand on the bench is kept moist by a trickle device fed by a small automatic cistern or sometimes directly from the water pipes. The other kind comprises a flexible plastic tube, into which very small side tubes can be fixed. The main tube is connected to the water supply and the side tubes are poked into the flowerpot containing the plant. There is thus a very slow trickle of water directly into the potting material. The great advantage of this latter type is that as the water is fed directly to the plant container the bench and its gravel or sand do not become too wet and algal and fungal growth are not encouraged.

Humidity Control

Most orchids require a fairly damp atmosphere, and dry air can have serious effects on any plants other than those in the resting phase. Transpiration from the leaves of actively growing orchids and evaporation from the potting medium provide a considerable amount of humidity but, when the air temperature rises in the greenhouses in sunny spells, an increased

The dense forests of tropical Central America are characteristically very humid. Orchids such as Epidendrum criniferum, a Panamanian, Costa Rican and Peruvian species, require a very humid atmosphere when in cultivation and this may mean frequent damping down of the orchid house.

humidity is desirable. The traditional way of providing this was firstly to have one or more open water tanks in the greenhouse and secondly by 'damping down' the floor and other surfaces at intervals during the day. In winter, damping down by watering can or syringe is rarely necessary, but in the middle of summer it may be required six or more times a day. The development of mist spray apparatus has obviated the need for much of this manual work. The mist spray not only sprays a fine mist of water into the air, but it does so only when an automatic electronic 'leaf' sensing device activates it.

Ventilation

Even in an unheated greenhouse, growing only European or Asiatic 'alpine' orchids, the temperature in the daytime in the summer can reach up to 40°C (104°F) very quickly. To avoid overheating the air and damaging the plants, it is necessary to ventilate the greenhouse. Although greenhouses are not absolutely airtight and the air inside could never become completely devoid of carbon dioxide or oxygen, the relative proportion of these atmospheric gases can become unsuitable for optimum plant growth and, again, the way to avoid this is to ventilate. A certain amount of air movement is necessary in an orchid house to avoid local concentrations of stale or very damp air near an actively growing plant, and also air circulation by the correct use of ventilators avoids temperature differentials near the glass or the heating pipes. The traditional way of ventilating a greenhouse was to open and shut the ventilators as necessary, but today temperature sensing devices are available for automatically controlling the opening and shutting of ventilators. The usual practice is for the ventilators to be slightly open and the automatic device opens them wider when the temperature rises and closes them completely when the temperature drops lower than desirable. The advantages of setting the device to operate in this way is that under optimum temperatures there is always some air movement.

Heating

The very earliest greenhouses were heated by large stoves and were often called 'stove' houses. The cost of maintaining these stoves and the dangerous local overheating that they produced mitigated against their continued use and they were soon superseded by hot-water pipes. For well over a hundred years, until about 1950, the use of large diameter pipes with hot water circulating through them was the commonest means of greenhouse heating from the largest commercial orchid houses to the smallest back-garden type. The heat was supplied by a boiler set into the base wall of the greenhouse and regularly stoked with coal or coke. Today most large commercial greenhouses are heated by a small-bore circulating hot water system fired by an oil burner but the smaller 'amateur' greenhouses nearly all employ a cleaner, less labour intensive and more immediately adjustable system.

Oil heaters of the wick or vaporizing 'blue-flame' type are very popular in Europe, and of course there is no installation cost involved. An improvement on this type are the piped or bottled gas heaters, which produce very little soot and do not require re-fuelling so frequently.

In countries where electricity is relatively cheap, electrically heated pipes are used but they have the considerable disadvantage of causing uneven heating. The thermostatically controlled fan heater is a very common type used today, and this has the advantage of assisting ventilation and air circulation as well as heating. Fan heaters can be expensive to run, but there is very little heat wasted with them and the problems of temperature gradients are obviated.

Lighting

All green plants require light as the energy source for chemically converting atmospheric carbon dioxide and water into carbohydrates high in chemical entry. As a general rule, orchids, especially those epiphytes from the dark rain forests, do not require as much light for successful growth as do many tropical plants. However, each day some light is essential, especially during the actively growing and flowering seasons. In the summer in the temperate zone of North America and Europe the day length and light intensity is amply sufficient for orchids but, as autumn and winter approach, it is essential for the flowering of certain species to have additional light. Colour-balanced fluorescent tubes or mercury vapour lamps

Pescatorea cerina is a Central American species grown especially for its very fragrant flowers. Sphagnum makes an ideal covering for the compost in which this orchid is grown.

are available for greenhouses and are well worth instaling in even the smallest type. They can be manually operated but time-switches or light sensitive photo-electric cells are often installed so that the system will operate even when the owner is absent.

Control systems
Greenhouse equipment can be installed and operated by any competent gardener but a warning must be added that even the simplest electrical systems should be inspected by a qualified electrician before use. If the greenhouse is fully automated with electrical controls for humidity, ventilation, heating and lighting and perhaps even pest controls, the electrical wiring and control panels can be a very complex installation

and it is essential that professional advice is sought from the very beginning to ensure safe and efficient working.

Potting containers and media

Orchids are divided into two categories for growing purposes, namely epiphytes and terrestrials. As a general rule, terrestrials are grown in a normal inorganic soil whereas epiphytes should be either grown on bark to simulate their natural habitat or in a fibrous potting medium.

Terrestrial orchids, such as *Eulophia*, many *Calanthe* species and hybrids, *Disa*, *Habenaria* and

The genus Cirrhopetalum *is closely allied to the more numerous genus* Bulbophyllum. C. robustum, *a native of New Guinea, requires warm and* humid conditions and is best grown in compost mixed with sphagnum moss. The flowers of this species have an **unpleasant smell.**

Pleione species, will thrive in any normal greenhouse potting soil provided that a considerable amount of fibrous material is added to it. In all cases the potting medium must be well drained and never compacted and airless. The soil can be in a traditional fired clay pot, a plastic pot of any shape, a wooden box or many plants can be grown together in a very large container or even in a built-in bed in the greenhouse.

The majority of the most popular and bizarrely floriferous orchids are epiphytes and for them to grow properly and freely produce flowers they must be correctly potted. The container is not so very important and although the clay or plastic flowerpot is still very widely used, the potting medium can be in a box or a lath basket. Some growers have reported successful results from growing epiphytes in fine nets or even stockings suspended from the roof of the greenhouse. It is the potting medium which is the most important factor in the successful growing of epiphytes. The composition of the medium is not so relevant as the way in which the plant is held in the medium. There must be very adequate aeration for all orchid roots and the mixture must never be too tightly packed around the plant. The material must be long-lasting as orchids do not like frequent repotting and it must be able to provide the minimal mineral requirements necessary for good growth. It should never get waterlogged but must never dry out so much that it cannot be re-wetted immediately. Finally, it must be springy enough to support quite large plants in small pots. Orchid plants must never be 'over-potted', which means that they only give of their best when in a relatively small pot. This is another way in which orchids are unique among greenhouse subjects!

There is no single substance which has all the necessary desirable properties, but by combining several materials very good results are obtainable. Traditionally epiphytic orchids were potted in osmunda fibre, which is the root fibres of the royal fern, *Osmunda regalis*. In most ways it is the best potting medium, needing very little additional material and having considerable longevity. However, its very high price, and the fact that collecting it in large commercially desirable quantities is leading to its extinction, mean that it is rarely used today. Good substitutes for osmunda fibre are the fibrous roots of other ferns, and those of *Polypodium* species have been extensively used. However, this is not so strong as osmunda fibre and is not often used today as it too has become very difficult to obtain.

A good cheap potting material is sphagnum moss but it needs some more rigid material added to it in order for it to anchor the plants. It is quite inert chemically, holds water well, and can be used by itself for the establishment of seedlings.

Coarse peat, tree-fern trunks ground up and dried beech leaves have been used and with many orchids are quite successful. However, a recent and cheap addition to the list has proved very successful and that is the shredded bark of conifer trees. This 'fir bark' is available as a waste by-product of commercial forestry and its only disadvantage is that it decays fairly rapidly.

As additives to potting mixtures, many growers use broken brick, fine gravel and coke, charcoal and clinker and most mixtures benefit by this.

Since the advent of plastics as one of the commonest materials in domestic use, they have been used in many potting mixtures. They have the advantage of being extremely cheap as the fibrous, flake, granular or shredded forms are generally waste materials and off-cuts from a plastics manufacturing process. The fibrous forms simulate osmunda fibre very closely in their chemical inertness and spring resilience.

If space is at a premium in the orchid house, there is no need to use potting containers and media at all, as many epiphytic orchids will grow on 'rafts' of compressed fibre or on bark. In the wild epiphytes grow normally on the bark of trees so it is much more natural to simulate these conditions in the greenhouse. Ideally, if a big enough greenhouse is available, a living jungle tree should be grown and the orchids attached to it, but this is rarely practicable and usually pieces of bark from the cork oak are used. These can be suspended from the roof of the house or, as is often done today in orchid houses in botanic gardens or the larger private collections, 'trees' can be fashioned out of plastic and steel and concrete and covered with cork bark, to which the plants are attached.

How to Grow Orchids

The cultivation of any group of plants consists primarily of a series of operations carried out on a progressive or cyclical basis in an attempt to simulate as far as possible the normal average conditions of the plants' original natural home. Therefore, the first and most important step to take in growing orchids is to ascertain the natural growth conditions of the individual plants being cultivated. If the plants have been directly imported from the wild, it should be easy to come across this information first hand, but most plants come from another collection, either private or commercial, and many plants, such as the hybrids, never had a truly native home. In these latter cases reference should be made to the standard textbooks available but in many instances it is better to ask the donor or seller of the plant how he has grown it.

Armed with this knowledge of what each plant requires, it is now necessary to reach a compromise as to the sort of conditions that, firstly, you can afford to provide economically and physically and, secondly, that suit the majority of the plants you wish to grow. It must be remembered that it is rarely possible or desirable to grow a wide range of orchid plants in a single small house as they have such a wide range of optimum conditions to flower successfully. Although orchid plants have tolerance ranges of environmental conditions in which they will thrive or survive, it is not physically possible to include all these in one small controlled environment. Therefore, if you wish to grow a great variety of orchids, the greenhouse must be partitioned to provide a different temperature regime in each section.

Earlier sections have dealt with the choice of greenhouse and the range of equipment available, especially automatically controlled types suitable for the grower who cannot devote much time to the hobby. Suitable planting containers and growing media were also mentioned. It is now up to the grower to ensure that all this equipment is used correctly!

What follows deals with the basic routine care of orchids which, despite the automatic devices available, need at least weekly attention. Further sections are concerned with the propagation of plants and give a brief survey of the pests and diseases that may attack all the orchids in a poorly kept collection but are usually confined to very old or very young specimens.

General cultivation

The publication of books on orchid cultivation is becoming more and more a common event and soon they will be as numerous as books on vegetable or fruit growing. None of the books on orchid growing can deal with the exact individual requirements of all 12,000 cultivatable species and the tens of thousands of cultivars of hybrid grexes that man has produced. Nevertheless, orchids fall into relatively few well-defined groups as far as their cultivation requirements are concerned and, once the basic conditions for each group are provided, it needs only minor individual attention to satisfy most plants in that group.

The basic grouping of orchids is into epiphytic or terrestrial plants (see page 12) and these groups are subdivided according to whether or not the plants require an annual resting phase or, at least, whether they are subject to some seasonality in their natural home. This gives four main groups and in each group the plants should then be further subdivided into the temperature regimes most satisfactory for their successful growing and flowering. It is usual to consider orchids as needing either cool (16–21 °C/60–70 °F

Repotting young orchids.

summer day to 10°C/50°F winter night), intermediate or temperate (18–24°C/65–75°F summer day to 13–16°C/56–61°F winter night) or warm 21–29°C/70–84°F summer day to 18–21°C/64–70°F winter night) conditions.

Although it is perfectly possible to grow terrestrials and epiphytes together in one house (and, provided they are not too mixed up, to grow together those with, and those without, a distinct resting phase) it is not possible to successfully cultivate cool and warm plants in one house. The temperature and humidity can usually be controlled so that most cool and intermediate plants will grow well together, and the same is true of most intermediate and warm plants.

The growth requirements for all orchid plants are light, heat and soil and atmospheric moisture. Mineral nutrients are also necessary but by and large orchids have a very low requirement and much of their need is provided from the breakdown of their potting medium or from atmospheric dust and from watering. Liquid feeding with a specially formulated orchid nutrient or with a home-made mixture of dung, blood, hoof and horn or an inorganic formulation can be

beneficial, especially if applied as a foliar feed to the orchids' leaves. Nevertheless, there is still controversy as to whether or not orchids require feeding and, if in doubt, the wisest course to take is not to feed but water with rainwater.

It is not intended to delve more deeply into the so-called mystique of orchid growing in this book as space precludes this, but it must be stressed that provided the temperature never falls below the winter night minimum and the plant is in the right medium, orchids can withstand very much more abuse or misuse of cultivation than most greenhouse plants. However, this should not be taken as an excuse for unwarranted neglect.

Propagation

There are three ways in which orchid plants can be reproduced and all have their uses depending on the number of offspring required and the rate at which they are required. These three methods are division, mericulture and seed.

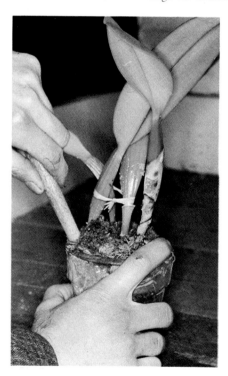 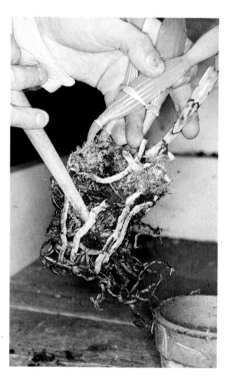 

Orchids are generally divided when they become too large for their containers. Left : a potting stick is used to lever the plant for repotting. Centre : the old compost is carefully teased away from among the roots. Right : fresh compost mixture is picked up in small amounts and arranged around the roots.

Division

Traditionally, orchids are divided when they become too large for their containers. This division is not usually into two or more equal parts but, when re-potting mature plants, the older pseudobulbs, called 'backbulbs', are removed and, if they have a small 'eye' shoot, they can be potted up separately. As a general rule, all pseudobulbous orchids should have no more than six or less than three pseudobulbs per potted plant. Some pseudobulbous plants, such as Pleiones, produce very small bulbs, which can be removed and grown to flowering size in two or three years.

With non-pseudobulbous orchids, the plants can be divided at root level, or side-shoots removed for potting up, provided they have at least one root. Many orchids produce complete miniature plants on their stems and these plantlets either drop off or are easily removed and can be potted.

Mericulture

Mericulture, or mericlonal propagation, or meristem culture, or micro-propagation, or whatever is the latest term for the tissue culture of orchids, has revolutionized the mass-production of the more popular species and hybrids. The technique of micro-vegetatively propagating has been patented but is carried out by most larger commercial orchid nurseries and by many amateurs.

Essentially this method of reproduction consists of surgically removing the actively growing points of side-shoots ('lateral meristems') and growing them in a nutrient culture medium. By carefully controlling the amount of nutrients and light available and by constant agitation or rotation, these meristems can be induced to divide into many more identical meristems. By further controlling the environmental conditions these meristems soon produce roots and leaves and these miniature plantlets can then be removed and pricked out and grown on as if they had resulted from the sowing of seed. Not all orchids are amenable to this type of reproduction but Cymbidiums, Calanthes, Dendrobiums, Miltonias, Odontoglossums and Oncidiums and, of course, hybrid genera involving these groups, have proved to be ideal subjects.

It is hoped that by refining the technique it will be

Left : when the roots are covered with new material and inserted into the pot, a potting stick is used to push the compost inward but not downward. Centre : the surface of the compost is trimmed with shears. Right : the plant ought to be sufficiently firm in the pot to be held up and gently shaken without the pot falling.

possible to reproduce all orchids easily in this way, but as yet *Paphiopedilum* and many of the Vanda group, such as *Phalaenopsis* and *Vanda* itself, are proving much less tractable. Research into the method is continuing as it is felt it could be of use in the reproduction of rare and endangered species that exist in such isolated populations or such small numbers that normal seed raising is not possible.

the orchid seeds were sown. For many years this method was disregarded as it is very time- and patience-consuming, but recently many orchids that have proved very difficult to propagate by any other method have been multiplied by this symbiotic means.

However, the usual method which is applied to the great majority of orchids and especially those of novel hybrid origin is the asymbiotic method. In this the

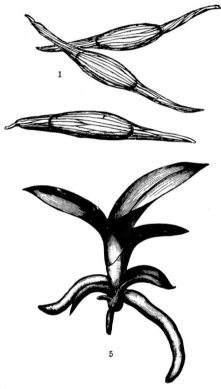

Seed

Propagation of orchids by seed is not at all like the normal method of seed sowing practised with all other plants. It is possible to raise orchids from seed sown in ordinary orchid potting media but this is a very chancy process. The reason why special techniques are required is because of the interdependence of orchids and the mycorrhizal fungus which is found in nearly all their tissues.

When this symbiotic relationship was first discovered, it was thought that fungus must be present for successful germination and the subsequent seedling growth. The fungus was isolated and grown in a specially prepared sterile culture medium, into which

germinating and growing medium is enriched by the addition of the mineral nutrients which would be provided in nature by the fungus. Many chemical formulae for these mineral nutrients have been devised: some are of well-known ingredients, such as calcium nitrate and ferric phosphate, but recently great success has been recorded when such complex mixtures as crushed bananas and fish meal have been added. Whatever formula is decided upon by trial and error and advice, all the ingredients, which always include a sugar, water and agar, are heated to sterilize the mixture. The acidity is then tested to ensure that the resulting brew is as near neutral as possible and then, when cooled, the seeds are sown. To preserve the

This illustration from Veitch's Manual of Orchidaceous Plants *(published in nine parts) shows the development of a* Cattleya *from seed to a two-year-old plant. 1. seeds* – *greatly enlarged ; 2. seedling (six months) – greatly enlarged ; 3. seedling (nine months) ; 4. seedling (twelve months) ; 5. seedling (sixteen months) ; 6. seedling (two years).*

sterility, the seeds themselves are sterilized before sowing and the test-tube or flask containing the germinating medium and the seeds is kept fungal-free by an absorbent cotton plug.

Sooner or later, and with many orchids this can mean over a year, the seeds germinate and, after a further and often considerable period, the minute seedlings are ready for transfer to a 'community' pot or box from where, after a long period again, they can finally be potted as young plants.

Attempts to accelerate this process include the culture of excised embryos and unripened, green-seed sowing.

Pests and diseases

Although orchids can be sensitive to untoward fluctuations in their growing conditions and respond by exhibiting symptoms of physiological disorder, such as bud-drop or leaf-shrivelling, they are remarkably hardy as far as pests and diseases are concerned. They are much less likely to suffer irreparable or lethal damage from fungal, bacterial, viral or insect attack than any other greenhouse plants, with the possible exception of succulents, such as cacti.

Provided the plants are grown in as ideal conditions as possible and were disease-free when first obtained, they can usually withstand attacks from the common pests such as aphids and the widespread disease caused by viruses. Even if they cannot repel or localize the infection, the development of a great range of chemical pesticides, fungicides, bactericides and insecticides makes the control and cure efficient and rapid.

A further development in the control of insect pests of orchid plants, especially the greenhouse white fly, is based on the fact that in the wild the pests themselves are preyed upon by their own pests, and so on, and the ecological maxim of diversity means stability comes into force. It is now possible to buy insects, generally as eggs to hatch, that are introduced to the infected greenhouse and attack and control the numbers of the pest.

Traditional pesticides are usually sprayed onto the infected plants but the advent of systemic formula-tions means that they can be watered around the plant, which is so very much safer and far less wasteful.

Another way of controlling the pests of orchids is by fumigation of the greenhouse. This can be carried out by lighting one of the proprietary 'bombs' and letting its pesticide-laden smoke penetrate every corner of the greenhouse, generally overnight. However, there is now a method of continually controlling pests by this means and that is by using an electrical device, into which are placed little tablets of different pesticides which are slowly vaporized into the atmosphere. There is one great problem with these electrical vaporizers, and that is that the continual presence of the pesticide in the atmosphere could cause the pest not only to become immune to its effects, but for resistant and more robust strains to be evolved. Also, as yet, we do not know the effect of prolonged exposure to the pesticide of the human beings tending the orchid plants and inhaling the treated air.

It has been found that many pests of orchids can be removed merely by washing them off with soapy water, which then drowns them. Rarely is very drastic action called for except when a weakly plant is found to be heavily infected by a virus, such as the Black Streak virus disease of Cymbidiums, when the only 'cure' to prevent the virus spreading is to burn the infected plant. Viruses are spread from one plant to another by sucking insects and can be transmitted by scissors and knives.

Some orchid pests and diseases are confined to one particular group of orchids but the commoner ones, such as aphids, red spider, scale insects, mealy-bugs and thrips have been found on all the more commonly grown plants. There are also larger pests which will feed on orchids as well as on almost any other plant, and in this group are included the ubiquitous cock-roaches and crickets which, even if banished from the greenhouse itself, soon re-invade from potting sheds and pipe ducting. Slugs and snails invading from the garden outside can also be a problem.

A major pest in orchid houses open to the public is a two-legged one called *Homo sapiens*, which re-moves plants, often complete with pot. The only real cure is to wire the pots securely to the benches.

The Orchid Trade

Today orchids can be purchased from a vast number of specialist growers. However, in the earliest days of the orchid cult, it was necessary to go out to the tropics and collect plants or, as actually happened, send out collectors for this purpose.

Today, most amateur orchid growers' collections start not from a purchase nor from plants collected abroad but with a gift from a fellow enthusiast. It is well known that once a small collection of orchids is established in a greenhouse that collection grows very rapidly in size and number of plants. Even if you are only reproducing orchids by the slow and traditional way of dividing plants when they become large, it does not take much time for all available shelf space to be utilized. More and more shelving, hanging baskets, annexes to the greenhouse, another greenhouse: all these are palliative measures, but sooner or later it becomes impossible to accommodate more plants. A neighbour has expressed interest in growing orchids after seeing your bulging greenhouse and therefore an obvious solution to reducing the bulge is to give away some plants. Unfortunately, this gesture on your part often aggravates the problems as the recipient will eventually give you some plants in exchange. The exchange of surplus orchid plants as collections grow and growers decide to specialize only in certain genera is the major way of building up and maintaining an orchid collection today.

This phenomenon of exchanging plants occurs wherever orchids are cultivated and leads to a further question as to the role of orchid nurseries. Commercial orchid nurseries flourish in certain parts of the world such as the United States of America and Australia but their growth has not kept in line with the growth of the amateur orchid-growing fraternity. The traditional role of orchid nurseries has been to introduce species into cultivation from the wild, and the great majority of the four or five hundred orchids most widely grown originated from nurseries which have built up stocks of proven quality from plants imported many years ago.

However, orchid nurseries that have concentrated on species have not been very successful financially during the last few years, as increasing competition has been encountered from 'direct export' companies in the tropics. There are serious objections to the destructive activities of these companies, but by undercutting the prices charged for orchids by traditional nurseries they have captured much trade. The ever-increasing exchanging of orchid plants has also had an effect on the viability of smaller nurseries.

The really successful orchid nurseries, if success can be judged by the size and number of their greenhouses, are those that concentrate on orchid hybridization and the promotion and selling of the results of their breeding programmes. With the advent in many countries of legislation giving patent rights to the breeders of new hybrids, the breeding nurseries' trade can be legally protected. The Plant Varieties and Seeds Act of 1964 provided for the setting-up of the Plant Variety Rights Office, and today there is a scheme in Britain granting breeders' rights to *Cymbidium* cultivars. The advantages for the holder of plant-breeders' rights to any cultivar are that he has a legal right in his new variety and can grant licences for the use of the new variety in return for royalties. In the United States originators of all sorts of plants are protected by the Plant Patent Amendment to the Patent Act.

The large orchid nurseries not only produce highly desirable orchid hybrids but, by means of the modern technique of meristem culture, are able to produce

The well-known Hawaiian orchid-breeder Oscar Kirsch raised Phalaenopsis Palmyra *in 1968, using as parents Grace Palm and the species* Phal. amboinensis.

thousands of identical plants very quickly. Thus the real value of orchid nurseries today is their ability to produce good quality hybrid plants in the quantity and at the price which will enable most growers to participate in cultivating them.

Although the great majority of plants in enthusiasts' collections have been obtained by donation, exchange or purchase and, of course, the grower's own personal efforts of seed-raising and vegetative reproduction, a certain number are still obtained by gathering them in the wild. This method could be increasing because of the popularity and relative cheapness of package holidays in tropical orchid-growing countries, such as the West Indies.

Commercial orchid growers

In the eighteenth century, when people in Europe first became aware of the treasures of the tropical forests of Asia and America, most of the orchids grown in greenhouses were introduced by explorers, sea captains and returning officers from the colonies. Some of the richest landowners sent out plant-collectors and, among the many plants they brought back, there were often orchids. Unfortunately, a lack of knowledge of the plants' native habitats and the inability to simulate the conditions which were known, led to most orchid plants surviving for only a short period.

The orangery, famous examples of which are still found today in such parks and gardens as those at Kew and Versailles, was the first home for imported tropical orchids, but the heated atmosphere which prevailed in them in the winter was far too dry for all but a few species to survive. However, in the 1820s a revolutionary new method of heating greenhouses by hot water circulating through large-bore cast-iron pipes provided more easily controllable and more suitable conditions for cultivating tropical orchids. At the same time the major heating material, coal, became much cheaper and much more widely available because of the extension of the canal and railway network. Thus, the basic essentials for orchid growing under glass were available and the ever-increasing exploration of Europe's tropical orchid-growing

colonies led to an ever-increasing flow of living orchids to most European countries.

It soon became profitable for nurserymen to employ their own collectors in the tropics, and in this context note must be made of the pioneers of commercial orchid growing in England, Messrs. Conrad Loddiges of London. In the next forty or fifty years many other firms were established, such as those of James Veitch, Hugh Low and Sander. In Belgium, France and Germany many similar were established but, unfortunately, the many wars in the next eighty years were responsible for the demise of most of them. Changing fashions, crippling tax burdens and a multitude of

Cymbidiums are popular orchids with commercial growers because they require relatively little heat and flower freely.

other factors, such as oil costs, have meant that today all the British orchid nurseries founded in the last century have also disappeared. The very last to go, Messrs. Black and Flory of Langley in Buckinghamshire, were direct descendants of the famous firm of Messrs. Veitch of Exeter.

The latter half of the nineteenth century saw an unprecedented growth in orchid nurseries, which imported millions of plants each year. Often the plants were sent directly to London by freelance collectors, who arranged for them to be sold at orchid auctions, where they could reach prices of over 100 guineas per plant. Messrs. Prothero and Morris of

London were famous orchid auctioneers, and their well-illustrated coloured catalogues are now collectors' items which can themselves fetch high prices at auctions!

Orchid hybrids

In 1856, in one of Veitch's greenhouses, there flowered the first man-made orchid hybrid, *Calanthe* Dominyi (*C. masuca* × *C. furcata*), and by 1871 seventeen hybrids were listed. This gentle trickle of man-made plants soon changed to a flood, and when Sander's *Complete List of Orchid Hybrids* was published in 1946 over 15,000 were recorded. Today the number of new hybrids is increasing by nearly a thousand each year.

These hybrid plants revitalized the orchid nursery trade in the early years of this century, when the amateur grower's appetite for species had apparently become rather jaded. The high prices paid for orchid species in the early days of importation were eclipsed by the 1,000 guineas or more often realized for the latest hybrid.

Orchid nurseries flourished on growing species and producing hybrids, but nurserymen of the more entrepreneurial type were always looking for further markets, and they soon found that the sale of cut-flowers could be profitable. Orchid growing for the cut-flower trade was established during the latter half of the last century but reached a peak in the Edwardian era and up to the outbreak of the First World War. The 1920s and 1930s saw a brief revival, but the fuel restrictions of the Second World War and the austerity afterwards had some effect. Since that time the availability of out-of-season roses, carnations and chrysanthemums, for example, and the importation of orchid blossoms from the Far East, has very seriously affected the home-growing of cut-flowers. Today the trade is mainly for funeral wreaths and wedding bouquets.

The trade today

Although today there are hundreds of commercial orchid-growing establishments in the more developed countries and an ever-increasing number becoming established by countries of the third world, it is in the United States of America that the trade has reached

such a size and status as to be considered a major industry. On glancing through the expensive fully colour-illustrated catalogues produced by American orchid nurseries, it is impossible not to be impressed by the range of plants that are available. In many ways it is surprising that the plants are so cheap, with the prices for most species and hybrids of the more popular genera and hybrid genera ranging from about $7.50 to $250. These prices may seem high for individual plants, but the increase in prices over the last hundred years has been negligible compared with the increases in every other sector of trade.

A major reason why prices are relatively stable is that new methods of propagation of orchids, such as meristem culture, have enabled growers to produce enough plants of a particularly desirable cultivar to satisfy the demand. Improvements in seed raising have enabled growers to review and evaluate the results of breeding programmes much more quickly than in the past. Plant growth in the nursery is much more easily controlled by the careful manipulation of temperature and light regimes so that the plants can be available at the peak demand times, such as Christmas and the early spring. In much of the United States, especially in the warm and wealthy southern states, orchids are grown with the minimum of artificial heating and have supplanted other garden subjects as the most popular plants. Therefore, the supply and demand side of the orchid trade have grown in harmony to produce the vast enterprise that orchid-growing now is in the United States.

Most of the orchid nurseries sell not only flowering-size plants but flasked seedlings and very young mericlones. They offer seed-raising and green-pod culture services for the amateur hybridist's own efforts at producing new plants. Much of their sales income comes from accessories, such as books, corsage-making supplies, fertilizers, fungicides, insecticides, labels and potting containers and media, and they may be associated with the suppliers of greenhouses specially designed for orchid growing. Flourishing export trade to many other countries also contributes to the overwhelming world dominance of the United States of America in the orchid-growing industry.

The great increase in fuel oil prices in the mid-1970s had a temporary economic effect on the orchid-growing trade throughout the world and this has now led to a more permanent effect. Before the price rise at least half of the orchids grown in the temperate countries required warm or intermediate greenhouse conditions, but since then growers' preferences have been for the species and genera that thrive at lower temperatures. In Britain, ever since the Second World War and its aftermath of scarce and expensive heating fuels, the cooler growing plants have been foremost in people's collections. In fact the enthusiasm for Cattleyas started to wane in the 1920s, when Mr. H. G. Alexander produced his famous grex *Cymbidium* Alexanderi and its world-renowned clone 'Westonbirt'. Massive *Cymbidium* breeding programmes have followed, and although only 34 species have been involved as parents, there are many more registered hybrids in *Cymbidium* than in *Cattleya*, which has about the same number of parent-worthy species.

Another change occasioned by high fuel prices is a simple physical one from large greenhouses that require a lot of heating to smaller ones that require less fuel. This has meant that smaller plants are becoming more popular than larger plants and again the genus *Cymbidium* and its species and hybrids has been to the fore. By using the smaller-flowered *Cymbidium* species, such as *C. devonianum* and *C. pumilum*, as parents in hybridization programmes, a range of so-called miniature Cymbidiums has been evolved. *Cymbidium* Dingledon (*C.* Alexanderi × *C. devonianum*) was the first 'miniature' Cymbidium raised as far back as 1933 but it was not until *C.* Minuet (*C. insigne* × *C. pumilum*) was produced in 1942 that they started to become popular. Since that time many hundreds of similar hybrids have been produced.

As well as plants with a lower temperature requirement and more compact growth, the trend of many orchid nurseries is towards offering plants that give good value for money by flowering more than once a year. The hybrid genera *Doritaenopsis* and *Ascocenda* frequently produce cultivars with more or less continuous flowering and a new race of Paphiopedilums with twice- or thrice-yearly flowering is being produced.

Undoubtedly the commercial orchid trade as a

Cymbidium *Alexanderi* 'Westonbirt' *is a product of one of the most successful and best-known orchid hybrids. In 1911,* C.

Eburneo-lowianum was crossed with the pale-rose C. insigne *to give* C. Alexanderi, *the forerunner of many of today's plants.*

Above : Brassolaeliocattleya *is the name given to the hybrids derived from* Brassavola, Cattleya *and* Laelia. Blc. *Veronica Chastenay is a hybrid between* Blc. *Nanette and* Cattleya trianaei *and was first raised in New York by the Arcadian Rose Gardens in 1945.*

Opposite : this traditionally arranged exhibit of Paphiopedilum *hybrids at a flower show demonstrates the great variety of floral forms and colours that have been derived from a relatively small number of natural species by interbreeding under man-made conditions.*

whole will weather economic storms and the demands of changing fashion in a conservation-conscious world, but the fate of individual firms is by no means so certain. The amateur grower will not suffer, but to obtain the right plants at the right price it may be necessary to send halfway across the world rather than patronize the local orchid nursery.

Orchid breeding

It is impossible to write very much about the growing of orchids without referring to orchid hybrids and orchid breeding. More new hybrids of orchids are produced every year than in all the other decorative plant groups put together, and the Royal Horticultural Society, which acts as the International Registration Authority for Orchid Hybrids, employs a Registrar of Orchid Hybrids full time to record the thousand or so new hybrids registered each year.

The first successful attempt at orchid breeding was in 1856, when Messrs. Veitch's nursery announced the successful flowering of *Calanthe* Dominyi (*C. furcata* × *C. masuca*). Today orchid hybrids are made by large and small orchid nurseries and by amateur orchid growers throughout the world. A glance at the early listings of hybrid orchids showed that most were raised in Europe, and especially in England, but in the last thirty years the United States of America has been in the forefront. Even the tropical countries, with their own decorative native species being grown in other parts of the world, have started breeding programmes to combine into one plant the most desirable facets of several of their native species. In 1929 the Singapore Botanic Gardens produced their first hybrids and this led to the present situation in which Thailand, Malaysia and Japan have overtaken the European countries in the number of new hybrids they are producing each year.

Orchids are much more amenable to hybridization than other groups of plants in that not only do two species in a genus cross easily with each other to produce fertile offspring which can then be back-crossed to either parent or crossed with a third species to produce yet another hybrid; but species and hybrids from different genera can also be crossed. There are many bi-, tri-, quadri-generic hybrids, and at

Odontioda *is a bigeneric hybrid between* Cochlioda *and* Odontoglossum. Odontioda *Ingera was raised in a British nursery,* Charlesworth's, *in 1956.*

least two quinque-generic (i.e. five genera) hybrids have been registered.

If two species are crossed, the resulting plant, called a primary hybrid, has characters generally intermediate between those of the parents, although each individual offspring plant will be slightly different from all others and some will be more like one parent than the other. When this primary hybrid is then crossed with a second hybrid, the resultant offspring can exhibit a much greater range of both colour and form than either parent. If the parent hybrids are of different generic constitution, such as when two distinct bigeneric hybrids are crossed, the progeny can have many features that were hidden in the parents. It is this repeated crossing of plants that can have ten or more species in their genetic constitutions, from two, three, four or even five different genera, that is producing the enormous range of plants that are widely available today.

Many amateur growers are under the mistaken impression that to cross orchids is a very complicated and time-consuming process. Much time is needed but this is all waiting time, waiting for the seed capsule on the female parent to mature. The actual process of crossing the parents is very simple although, of course, unless the right equipment is available, the seed germinating can be complicated. Nevertheless, if these latter facilities are not at hand, most commercial orchid nurseries or specialist commercial orchid laboratories offer a seed-raising service for a small fee. If the amateur hybridist is too impatient to wait many months for the hybridized seed capsule to mature and ripen its seeds, some orchid nurseries offer a 'green-pod' culturing service. In this process the unripened embryo is 'germinated' and the cost is only marginally higher than traditional seed sowing.

The first step in 'home hybridizing' of orchids is to select carefully the parent plants to be crossed. Many growers make the error of trying to cross almost every plant in their collection with every other plant. They

Previous page : Odontioda *Florence Stirling is a hybrid between* Odontioda *Astoria and* Oda. *Melina. One of the most popular cultivars is* 'Lyoth'.

Above : Paphiopedilum *seedlings, their parentage carefully labelled, raised in community pots.*

are inevitably disappointed when the apparently ripe capsules produce non-viable seed, or if good seed does result the subsequent plants are quite worthless in that they have combined the worst rather than the best features of the parents. The parent plants must not only have flowers of quality with features that could be profitably combined but they must be of vegetative vigour, tolerant of a wide range of environmental conditions and free-flowering with no undesirable characters such as premature bud-drop.

A problem can arise when a grower decides that two plants should be crossed and they flower at different times of the year so that the physical transfer of the pollinia to the stigma becomes impossible. One way out of this problem is to manipulate the growing conditions of either or both parents so that they produce at least some flowers simultaneously, but there is a much easier solution and that arises from the discovery that pollinia can be stored for several months with only a minimal loss in potency. The only requirement is that the pollinia must not be stored in too damp conditions that encourage fungal and bacterial growth or in too dry an atmosphere that dries out the pollen. If the pollinia are freeze-dried, it is sometimes possible to store pollinia for even longer times.

The physical transference of pollinia from the male parent to the receptive stigmatic surface of the female parent is a very simple task. The pollinia are detached with tweezers or a piece of wood like a cocktail stick and placed on the stigma, where they readily adhere. In some orchids the pollination is immediately followed by fertilization but in most species the latter process occurs several months later. The fact that the female flower wilts and withers when the pollen is transferred to its stigma is not evidence that fertilization has occurred. The ovary of the female flower will often swell on pollination but unless fertilized no viable seeds will result.

The would-be breeder of orchids may be somewhat disillusioned by the time taken to know whether or not a crossing has produced seed and then by the inordinate time taken for seed ripening and germination. However, most good gardeners have patience and the amateur hybridist hopes another plant the quality of *Cattleya* Bow Bells is in the making.

Orchids from the wild

The ultimate source of all orchids is from the wild although with the hybrids which are so widely grown today it is their parents that once grew in the tropical forests.

In the early days of exploring for plants very few orchids were collected and the great majority of these did not survive the voyage to the conservatories of Europe. However, as the interest in exotic plants heightened and their needs in cultivation became better understood, more and more orchids were brought in from the wild.

A considerable number of orchid plants available today are divisions and seedlings from these early importations, but to cope with the demand fresh importations from the tropics are still being made. With greater sophistication in packing wild plants for transit and with the great speed of air transport, most wild plants collected today reach their destination in good condition.

Unfortunately, the phytosanitary import regulations of several countries kill many of these importations, which leads to a greater demand on the source of supply. For example, some countries (in order to prevent the unwitting introduction of plant diseases) insist that all imported orchids, as well as having a phytosanitary certificate from the exporting country, must be fumigated or dipped in insecticide immediately on arrival. As this fumigation can be methyl bromide gas under pressure, the effect on a young orchid plant is frequently lethal. These measures can be so draconian that one is forced to conclude that their imposition is an economic trade protection device primarily and a phytosanitary device secondly.

Although concern was expressed more than fifty years ago about the effect of these great importations of wild orchids into Europe and North America, the great majority of the public and orchid growers themselves knew and had always been taught that nature was ever fruitful! The attitude was that wild plants, as well as wild animals, were part of nature's bounty and that reproduction would make good any desecration.

However, slowly over the years, and spurred on by the knowledge that the world's human population was increasing at an ever-expanding rate, the concern for nature and natural resources, such as timber and fuel supplies, became more and more widespread. Politicians and economists, who previously thought that the only finite resources were men and money, suddenly realized that materials themselves were not in infinite supply.

European Conservation Year in 1970 and the oil shortages of the mid-1970s brought home to the whole world that the earth was not so bountiful in the face of the increasing onslaught on her resources. Botanists had been in the forefront of the 'doomsayers' for many years and wild orchids were given prominence as a natural resource that was disappearing at an alarming rate.

Of the 18,000 or more species presently accepted in the orchid family, perhaps a third or even a half of these are threatened with outright extinction by the end of the century, or at the very least there is sure to be a very serious reduction in numbers of plants in each species. The reduction in numbers could be so great that the genetic potential of the species would be severely limited, and thus, only able to cope with a limited range of environmental conditions, it would be bound to die out sooner or later.

The plight of the orchids was such that the International Union for the Conservation of Nature and Natural Resources (IUCN – a subsidiary body of UNESCO) through its Survival Service Commission, set up a study group to investigate the situation. As a result of the group's findings and the fact that many other plant families were similarly threatened, IUCN established the Threatened Plants Committee, which has a full-time staff monitoring the well-being of threatened plants and taking action where necessary.

Protection and conservation today

A Convention requiring export and import licences for all orchids, and for all endangered plants and animals, has been internationally agreed and is fully operative by enactment in the majority of orchid supplying and 'demanding' countries. Many commercial orchid nurserymen have expressed great concern over the restrictions placed on the international trade

In the wild, orchids are threatened by changes to their natural habitat and indiscriminate collecting. Dendrobium smilliae, for example, from Northern Queensland, Australia, has been over-collected by private and commercial collectors because of its attractive and unusual flowers, which have given it the common name jelly bean orchid.

77

in orchids by this *Convention on International Trade in Endangered Species of Wild Fauna and Flora*, especially as it is only the orchid family that is completely protected by including all orchid plants within its jurisdiction. It was felt necessary to include all orchid plants as experience has shown that by only applying the legislation to some species it is very easy to smuggle in protected species under the name of an unprotected species. Experienced orchid botanists find it impossible to recognize the identity of an unflowered seedling of most orchids and it would have been grossly unfair on the government officials at airports and seaports to expect them to decide whether or not a small orchid plant was species A, which was endangered and therefore protected, or species B, which was very common.

It is proving difficult to explain to many commercial orchid growers that a rigidly controlled and licensed orchid trade now is essential if there are to be any orchids left to trade in by the end of the century! However, it must not be thought that

unscrupulous and unthinking orchid importers are fully responsible for the decline in the variety and numbers of wild orchids. Probably far more species are lost by forest clearance, the drainage of wetlands and pollution caused by industry and agriculture than by the over-collecting of orchids for commercial or private gain.

The establishment of large National Parks, nature reserves and areas of 'protected wilderness' help to protect orchids and other plants. In England the very rare lady's slipper orchid (*Cypripedium calceolus*) is known in the wild by only two plants but these are protected by a 24-hour-a-day guard for the summer period before, during and after they have flowered. New techniques of orchid propagation and the establishment of seed banks for orchids are two very positive methods of protecting wild orchids from extinction but the final battle will be won only when all concerned with orchids realize that it is in everybody's best interest to protect the great range of species that form the world's largest plant family.

Above : the lady's slipper orchid, Cypripedium calceolus *(left), is extremely rare in Britain and disappearing throughout its range as a result of up-rooting and picking. The* *marsh helleborine,* Epipactis palustris *(right) is commoner but rapidly becoming extinct because its marshy habitats are being drained.*

Opposite : the dune early marsh orchid, Dactylorhiza incarnata, *subspecies* coccinea, *is another European orchid, which occurs mainly in the damp* *'slacks' of coastal sand dunes ; it is becoming quite rare as the dunes become damaged by tourism, car parking and sand removal.*

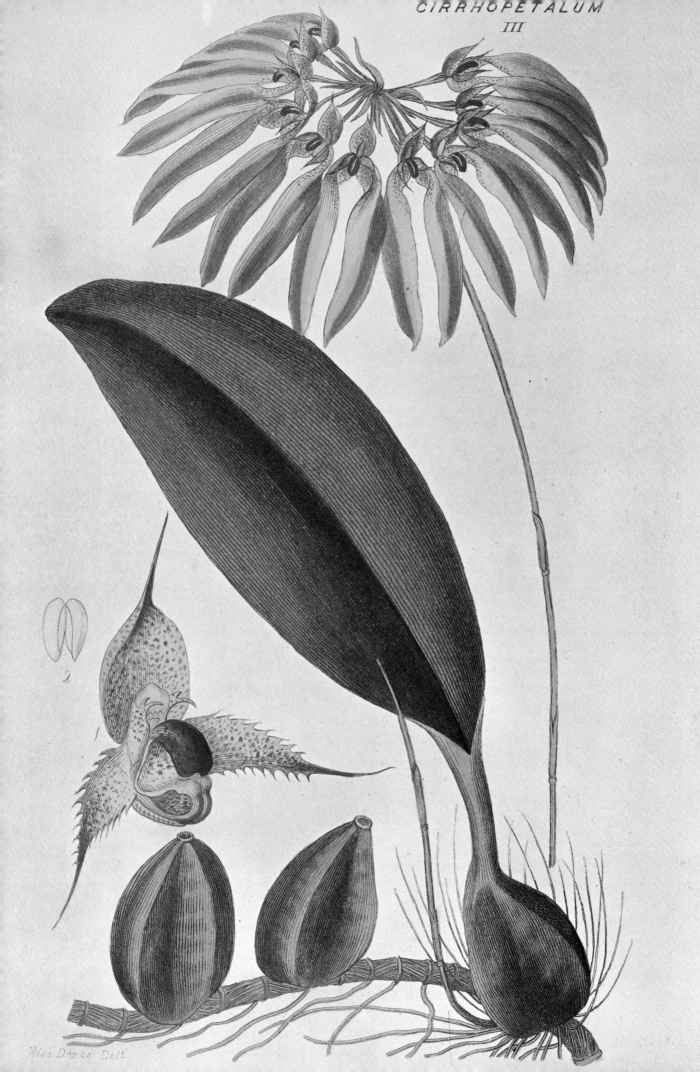

Where to Find out About Orchids

An essential feature distinguishes a passing interest from an absorbing hobby and that is the hobbyist's incessant quest to discover more about his subject. Orchid hobbyists, or orchidists as they are commonly called in the United States, are certainly no exception, and the orchid cult has given rise to a vast 'data bank' about orchids.

Native orchids

Apart from the actual hobby of cultivating exotic orchids, the interest in the family often extends to finding out more about local, native orchids. Perhaps it was the early eighteenth-century botanists who first searched the countryside around their homes for orchids and compiled notes on their habits, habitats and rarity, but soon the orchid growers followed them. Native orchids are always much duller than exotic species but, nevertheless, have an innate interest that exotics can never possess. In England the wild orchids were avidly searched for, usually picked and often uprooted for transplanting. When the British Empire was in its heyday, the exiled colonial civil servant may well have dreamed about the native orchids around his former English home and, perhaps to alleviate his homesickness, he soon made forays into the orchid-rich jungles around his new home. The contribution of expatriates from Britain, Belgium, Holland, France and Germany to our knowledge of the world's flora and fauna has never been stressed enough. The British East India Company, founded in 1600 to control the trade with India, even had its own herbarium and collectors in India, and the results of their work are inestimable. Orchids always figured largely in the explorations carried out by civil servants and traders.

Orchid-hunting, not necessarily to grow or to collect but just to ascertain what orchids there are present, is today a favourite pastime among people from all walks of life and in all countries. Some hunters are botanists, many are growers but many are just interested in wild things, animals and plants in a desultory way, until the first occasion they find an orchid, when their enthusiasm is suddenly born. They soon become orchid hunters and realize that it is one of the easiest, and can certainly be the cheapest, way of finding out more about orchids.

Botanic gardens and parks

The city dweller may have to go a long way from home to find orchids, although this is certainly not strictly true of big cities like London, New York, Paris, Tokyo or Edinburgh. Orchids may not grow as weeds on rubbish piles or alongside transport routes in cities, but very exotic species and the latest additions to the range of hybrids may be very close at hand. The reference, of course, is to the collections of living orchids found in botanic gardens and municipal parks throughout the world. A list of botanical and other gardens throughout the world with orchid collections appears as Appendix D.

In the tropics local orchids may be growing on trees already in the area and the orchid grower has merely to tie a few introduced species and hybrids to the same trees to enhance the collection. Tropical gardens featuring orchids are being created all the time, and can be not only a valuable commercial or municipal asset but can greatly contribute towards the educating of the public in the conservation of species threatened with extinction.

Most of the largest botanic gardens of the temperate world were established a hundred or even two hundred or more years ago. Since their earliest days, these

Cirrhopetalum umbellatum *is a species unusual in that it extends throughout the old world tropics, from Africa through Asia and northern Australia as far east as Tahiti. This illustration is a* *good example of the early work of the nineteenth-century botanical artist Miss F. A. Drake.*

gardens have cultivated orchids and many of them carry out research into new growing methods and potting media. The botanic garden at Singapore initiated an orchid hybridizing programme many years ago using species native to South-East Asia and this was the beginning of today's vast orchid breeding, cultivation and exporting industry in Singapore and Malaya.

The basic idea of a botanic garden is that as great a range of plants as possible is grown for display to the public and for research and reference. To see a great variety of orchids every orchid hobbyist must pay a visit to as many botanic gardens as possible. Some plants succeed in the care of a botanic garden whereas others soon die, this depending on several reasons such as the various skills of the growers and the situation of the garden itself. This means that the orchid collection will be always changing as some plants die and are removed and fresh importations take their place. Some orchid plants flower almost throughout the year and the tropical American *Scaphosepalum ochthodes* always has at least one flower open on its wiry rachis. Other orchids, such as species of the American genus *Sobralia* and the Asiatic *Ephemerantha*, have flowers that open for a day or even just a few hours. In contrast the New Guinean species *Dendrobium stratiotes* is often used as a parent in hybridizing not only for its external floral features but as its individual flowers will last up to nine months if not pollinated.

Exhibitions

Exhibiting orchids is covered on pages 87–8, but here I would like to point out that much can be learned about orchids from *visiting* flower shows. Most of the larger flower shows have classes for orchids, as individual plants, as small groups and often as large co-operative amateur growers' or trade exhibits. The national orchid societies in each country and most of the regional and local societies as well hold at least one annual orchid show. Some of the larger societies, such as those in the heart of amateur and commercial orchid growing in California, hold several major shows every year. At some shows there will be an overwhelming number of *Cymbidium* hybrid plants but at another the majority may be Cattleyas or Vandas.

Orchid nurseries

All the countries in which orchids are grown have at least one commercial orchid nursery selling orchids to amateur growers and nearly all of these welcome visits by newcomers to orchid growing. You will see not only the plants they normally sell but almost certainly there will be many new and old hybrids and unusual species which are not catalogued. The new hybrids will not be available until they have proven their performance but the old hybrids and many of the species could be sold to you for a relatively small sum.

Hunting for orchids, visiting orchid collections at botanic gardens, going to orchid shows and contacting orchid nurseries are just four ways of finding out more about orchids. The following sections deal with the role of orchid societies, exhibiting orchids, orchid literature and orchid illustrations, but this is not the end of the list! Orchids have been used as the source of inspiration by several artists, ranging from sculptors to porcelain designers and jewellery makers. In fact many orchid growers of my acquaintance as well as collecting orchid plants to grow, books to help them grow the orchid plants and photographs and drawings to record the result of their growing efforts, also collect orchid-decorated crockery or golden brooches, or use the flowers of the plants they grow to create floral decorations. These latter can be either what is called 'floral art', which is table and similar arrangements, or it can be 'floristry', which is the making of bouquets, corsages, button-holes or occasionally floral 'tributes', such as wreaths or crosses.

In the future there are surely several other features of orchids that will be exploited. A guess would be the more widespread use of orchid scents to produce perfumes that can be bottled. Another suggestion could well be the chewing of parts of orchid plants to ascertain if they possess any hallucinatory chemicals!

Orchid societies

Orchid-growing and orchid-hunting in the wild are obsessive pastimes and usually lead to associated hobbies such as orchid-photography, orchid-book collecting and orchid-illustration collecting. The

Above : Sobralia
xantholeuca *is a
very short-lived flower of a
long-lived plant from
tropical America. This
illustration is from* Curtis's
Botanical Magazine.

Overleaf : Cattleya *Alice
Shirai is a hybrid produced
by crossing the world-famous*
Cattleya *Bow Bells with*
Cattleya *Snow Song.*

orchidist is always striving to find out more about the plants to which he or she has become addicted. The orchid grower cannot go on forever adding more and more plants to his collection; the orchid photographer is not satisfied merely to amass a larger and larger collection of transparencies; the hunter wishes to impart the more spectacular aspects of his travels; the book and illustration collector is dying to show his treasures to a wider audience. They join orchid societies, of which there are nearly twenty in Great Britain, over two hundred in the United States, and dozens in such other orchid-growing countries as Australia, South Africa, Canada and Japan.

To co-ordinate their activities in Britain, Australia and South Africa, national Orchid Councils have been established, but in the United States most societies are affiliated to the American Orchid Society. On an international scale the International Orchid Commission is co-ordinating various aspects of orchid cultivation, such as the registration and naming of man-made hybrids, and through the associated World Orchid Conferences representatives of nearly all the world's orchid societies meet to discuss the science and love of orchids and hold exhibitions.

It is interesting to visit the monthly meetings of local orchid societies. The national societies and the specialist groups, such as the International Phalaenopsis Society and the Cymbidium Society of America, must deal with 'matters orchidaceous' on a formal level but the activities of the local societies, wherever they are, are formal only in that their format is very similar. The meeting starts with a talk on some aspect of orchids or orchid growing and is then followed by a 'table show' in which members of the society exhibit interesting or unusual plants which they have grown. The formula is inevitably successful and rarely changes except that on at least one occasion each year a meeting is held that is devoted entirely to showing orchids. Members of the non-orchid-growing public and members from other orchid societies are also invited and may be invited to exhibit. Trade exhibits usually occupy a considerable proportion of the space

Among the best ways of learning about orchids and their cultivation is through visiting local flower shows and by joining an orchid society.

and are a very important way of introducing the latest discoveries, whether they are recently imported species or new man-made hybrids.

An orchid society is a good place to obtain new plants, as any member sooner or later will be willing to exchange surplus plants such as those that have been found to reproduce very easily or, as sometimes happens, when the grower decides to concentrate on a particular type of orchid and wishes to rid himself of the remainder.

Nearly all orchid societies, whatever their size, are a good source of information by means of their published newsletters. The larger societies may publish a glossy monthly magazine full of colour plates and a well-balanced selection of serious scientific articles and those intended for growers and exhibitors of all degrees of competence. The *American Orchid Society Bulletin* is the foremost example of this type of journal and is subscribed to all over the world. There is nothing strictly analogous in England because the *Orchid Review* is an independent journal although it carries news from many of the larger orchid societies. The small society with less than fifty members will probably produce a quarterly duplicated two-sided news-sheet but by studying who wins most prizes and discovering their methods and by finding out which genera are most successful in your area, these modest publications are of great value in finding out more about orchids.

A list of the world's major orchid societies appears as Appendix C.

Exhibiting orchids

One of the functions of orchid societies, whether they are purely local or national, is to organize exhibitions of living plants. There are also international orchid shows such as those held in such places as London, Medellin (Colombia), Sydney and Bangkok in association with the World Orchid Conferences. Orchid shows are usually competitive but this is not invariably the case and some are held as showplaces for an orchid-growing area's wares. For whatever reason or wherever shows are held, they are always well worth attending, not only to see the plants them-

selves but to meet fellow orchid enthusiasts. If there are several trade stands present, it is very rewarding to be able to compare the excellence of cultivation and the range of plants they stock and, perhaps more important, to be able to compare their prices. Orders for plants to be delivered at the right season are always willingly accepted and there is a growing trend for more and more orchids to be sold at the show itself, a practice once frowned upon by many show organizers. The latest books on orchids, exhibitions of orchid paintings and photographs and even displays of greenhouses and aids such as heaters, ventilators, growing media, fertilizers and pesticides are at the larger shows. The annual show of the British Orchid Growers' Association at the Halls of the Royal Horticultural Society in London in March every year is attended by professional and amateur growers from all over the world. The regional orchid congresses in the United States serve a similar function.

There is always mixed feeling among orchid growers about the value or even the morality of the competitive showing of orchids. The reasoning behind competitive showing is complex but basically it is a combination of getting appreciation for time-consuming efforts in cultivation, as an appraisal of different cultural techniques, an approval of new trends in orchid fashions, judgement of the results of orchid hybridization programmes and the exposure, to a fresh and attentive audience, of rare and unusual species or new and interesting hybrids. The great range of orchid cultivars and species available today and the considerable number of cultural techniques that are practised in many parts of the world owe very much to the competitive showing of orchids at relatively small local shows. It should also be mentioned that competitive showing of any plants, or animals, or almost anything else in the world, is a very useful method of assessing and, more important still, of moulding public tastes.

How do you set about showing? The first essential is to find a show that will cater for orchids. This will probably be your local orchid society's monthly meeting's 'table' but could be your local firm's or club's or allotment society's annual flower show or, possibly, even a larger regional or national show. In any case you must make certain that there is a class in the show that is open to you as a competitor and to the type of plant that you are intending to exhibit. Almost certainly you are aware of and actually practise the next essential steps when you prepare your plants to bring to your meetings or even when a fellow orchid enthusiast comes to look around your greenhouse: it is no more than choosing the best-grown plant of a particular group, of greatest intrinsic beauty, interest and form, at its acme of perfection. The chosen plant is then packed in such a way that it travels unharmed, not forgetting, of course, to first clean the plant, removing any badly damaged or otherwise unsightly leaves, and to scrub the pot. The useful refinement of dressing the pot, usually by covering it with moss, is an easy technique to master. Not quite so easy is to learn how to 'hold back' flowers for a show some time in the future and to ensure that all the flowers on a spike are in full, but not too full, bloom at the same time and that the lower ones have not already withered and started to form capsules. Nevertheless, if you are successful in growing and flowering the majority of plants in your collection, the exhibition techniques are very quickly acquired.

Perhaps you may feel that you do not have any really interesting enough or sufficiently spectacular plants, hybrids or species, at just the right stage, in your collection to show as individual exhibits, although this may well be a condition caused not by your cultivation skills or imagined lack of them or by the vicissitudes of your greenhouse heating, watering or ventilation system or the weather, but by your reticence and modesty. However, there is no reason to believe that a real or imaginary lack of a suitable plant means that you cannot exhibit. Many shows have classes for a small group of plants, either of the same or related or even totally distinct genera. I must stress that even classes for individual plants are not judged solely on the rarity or novelty of the exhibits and this is even more true when you are showing groups of plants. In these cases it is very much more the evenness of your cultivation techniques that gains the awards and often the 'staging' (how you arrange them in the group) can influence a judge's decision.

With many growers their route to competitive showing is via contributing, on loan, a few of their plants and a few hours of their time, to a joint co-operative, usually society-organized, exhibit. If one does not wish to expose one's plants or cultural techniques to the critical assessment of judges, one can be fairly anonymous as a participant in contributing towards and helping to arrange a tableau-like group. The Orchid Society of Great Britain always has a co-operative exhibit at the Chelsea Flower Show in London and many are held in America.

Orchid books

The supposed and real rarity of many orchids, their odd behaviour and mysterious-looking flowers, and the many expeditions sent out to collect them have caused a vast number of books to be published about various aspects of the family. As with most topics, the literature can be divided into the good, the bad and the indifferent but, with orchids, a greater proportion fall into the first category than into the other two. Even some works which are indifferent in their content or presentation are usually good in that they succeed in communicating their author's enthusiasm for orchids. Some are bad as far as their illustrations are concerned but have an excellent text and in many an indifferent text is enlivened by a profusion of first-class colour photographs.

In the last century, before the advent of photographic reproductions in books, a generation of artists was commissioned to prepare illustrations for publications. In many cases the illustrations were printed as line-drawings and students and out-of-work artists were employed to hand-colour each plate in each copy of the book. *Curtis's Botanical Magazine*, which has appeared regularly since the end of the eighteenth century, employed this technique for over a hundred years of its existence and the early volumes are collectors' pieces today. At the present time the illustrations, and each issue always contains at least one orchid, are colour-printed, not from colour photographs but from a specially commissioned artist's painting.

Bateman's *Orchids of Mexico and Guatemala*, a magnificently produced volume weighing 13.5 kg (32lb) and measuring 53 cm × 74 cm (21 in × 29 in), is perhaps the supreme example of Victorian orchid-

Epidendrum alatum, *a Central American species, more correctly called* Encyclia alata, *has recently been crossed with* Laeliocattleya *hybrids to produce Epilaeliocattleyas.*

EPIDENDRUM ALATUM.

book production. A number of the colour plates are of exceptional artistic merit. Sander's orchid nursery was responsible for the four volumes of *Reichenbachia*, which, in the Imperial Edition, weighed 20 kg (44 lb) each, and which today can fetch several thousands of pounds per volume. The illustrations in this work were among the first to be fully colour-printed by lithograph.

Orchid books can be grouped into seven major types, viz. general accounts of orchids and orchidology, accounts (Floras) of the orchids of a particular region, generally a country or group of countries, monographs dealing with all the orchids of a group, generally a genus, books dealing with the biology and scientific aspects of orchids and orchid culture, accounts of orchid 'personalities', general books on orchid cultivation intended for the beginner and, finally, cultivation reference books for the advanced grower and including the stud-books of orchid hybrids. There is not room here to examine in any detail the vast wealth of orchid literature available today, and the enthusiast will in any case make his own choice according to his field and level of interest. However, two of these categories deserve special mention.

Orchid Personalities

The growers, breeders and researchers of orchids have a greater chance of achieving immortality than those concerned with other plants because their names can be used as the root of intergeneric hybrids. These names not only enter the literature of orchid books, periodicals and catalogues, but are accepted by all botanists and become recorded in such erudite books as the *Index Kewensis*. Hybrid genera with three genera involved are named either by combining parts of the names of the three genera, for example, *Brassolaeliocattleya (Brassavola* × *Cattleya* ×

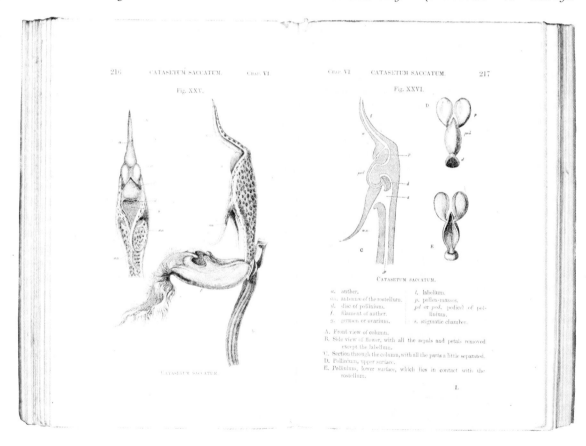

In his famous book The Various Contrivances by which Orchids are Fertilised by Insects, *Charles Darwin deduced the mechanism by which the* pollinia of the species Catasetum saccatum *are ejected at great speed when the rostellar 'antennae' are touched.*

Laelia) or by adding the suffix *ara* to the name of a person connected with orchids. For hybrids involving more than three genera it is obligatory to form names in this way. Thus we have, as examples, *Hookerara* and *Holttumara* honouring botanists, *Lewisara* and *Moirara* commemorating two internationally known amateur orchid growers, and *Sanderara* and *Scullyara* named after two leading firms of commercial orchid nurserymen. Over 150 orchidists have been honoured so far!

Perhaps because of this unique mechanism of commemorating orchid lovers very few books have been written on particular people concerned with orchids. Obituaries abound but full-scale books are very few and far between. The only one of international repute and decided value beyond the confines of the orchid world, is Arthur Swinson's *Frederick Sander, the Orchid King*, which deals with the rise not only of Sander himself but the entire ramifications of the mid- and late-Victorian cult of orchidomania. For short biographies Reinikka's *A History of the Orchid* should be consulted.

Cultivation Reference Books

Many of the books in this category were first published during the last century and have been periodically revised since that time, although some, such as the famous William's *Orchid Growers Manual* last published (edition 7) in 1894, are still being reprinted. Veitch's *Manual of Orchidaceous Plants* is another example and its value can be judged by the high prices copies reach in the auction rooms and antiquarian booksellers. Most present-day works deal with individual topics in depth, such as *Gardening Indoors Under Lights* (Kranz) and the *Orchid Judging Handbook* (British Orchid Council).

Finally, no survey of orchid books could be complete without mentioning the catalogues of orchid plants and sundries for sale that are regularly issued by the orchid nurserymen. Some are such expensively produced publications that the growers usually make a nominal charge. Even if you do not grow orchids, it is well worth getting a copy of the American firm Jones and Scully *Recommendations* which, although a catalogue, has over 325 colour photographs of orchid species and hybrids.

Orchid illustrations

Mankind has always attempted to control nature by reproducing aspects of it on a scale and of a substance that can be controlled and comprehended. The drawings of fierce beasts on the walls of prehistoric man's caves and the statuettes of many animals found in burial places are two well-known examples. The leaves of trees and shrubs have been used many times as the motifs for sculptures, medallions and coins. The flowers of many garden plants, especially roses and lilies, are constantly being used for the decoration of many household articles, such as china, wallcoverings and furnishing fabrics.

Orchids have been the subjects for relatively few such domestic or similar purposes, but as subjects for direct imitation they are very important. At the Botanical Museum of Harvard University there is a unique collection of sculptured glass orchid flowers, and at the Royal Botanic Gardens at Kew whole orchid plants have been depicted in coloured wax. A few years ago there was a fashion for gold brooches in the form of orchid flowers, especially those in the genus *Oncidium*. Ceramic orchids by O'Hara were recently on display in the Morland Gallery in London and were sold at incredibly high prices.

Orchids have been depicted at some time or other in nearly every artistic medium and in the case of some artists it has been the very carefully dried and preserved flowers of orchids that have been used in the final work. The embedding of various objects in a resinous plastic is a popular hobby today and it has been found that the essentially three-dimensional character of orchid flowers is particularly amenable to this type of preservation for ornamental purposes.

As subjects for painting, especially in watercolours, orchids have been excelled only by such widespread and available plants as roses. However, in the Middle Ages orchids were illustrated only as woodcuts and never appeared in the paintings of the great artists of the time. The German herbalist Otho Brunfels (1489–1534) included several European orchids in the woodcuts which adorned his works. Up to the middle of the seventeenth century about twenty orchid species had been illustrated and none were of great horticultural importance, but as the European explorers gradually penetrated into the tropics the accounts of their travels included an ever-increasing number of orchids.

In 1793 the first coloured illustration of an orchid was published and not surprisingly it was of the first tropical orchid to flower in Britain, *Helleborine americana* or as it is now more correctly called *Bletia verecunda*. It was, in fact, an early form of mezzotint and the colours of each plate printed were 'touched-up' with water-colours after printing. Very few colour-printed illustrations appeared after this for many years as it was found that much better and much more accurate and acceptable illustrations could be produced by printing in black and white and employing students to hand-colour them. In 1790 *Curtis's Botanical Magazine* was first published and was quickly joined by many imitators. It is unique among such journals in that it is still published today in very much the same format as nearly two hundred years ago when it first appeared, except that the very latest methods of colour printing are used today to reproduce accurately the colours of the artist's original work. The artists who painted for these magazines also produced many plates for other publications such as Floras and Monographs, and in many cases the author of a learned tome was also the illustrator. All botanical illustrators, and especially those that concern themselves mainly with orchids, have to be fully aware of the intricacies of the structure of orchid flowers, and it is because of their dual abilities as biological investigator and artist that the works they produced are so valuable today. Many of the illustrations of orchids produced in the last century by such people as Bauer, Bateman, Linden, Warner, Hooker, the incomparable Fitch, Woolward and Moon, to name only a very small proportion, are eagerly sought after today in bookshops and auction rooms by art collectors as well as by taxonomic botanists.

The twentieth century saw a great increase in orchid growing as a hobby to be carried on in a relatively small greenhouse in a suburban garden. This led to a corresponding increase in the publication of relatively cheap and simply written books on orchid growing and the majority of these were illustrated by equally simple line drawings.

At the same time botanists started to consolidate their knowledge of the floras of the tropics and many Floras and Monographs were published. These were not on the same lavish scale as those produced earlier by the nineteenth-century botanists but they were equally well illustrated with black and white line drawings. These works, published entirely for their scientific content and often produced and sponsored on an international basis, are appearing at a faster rate now than ever before, and many artists are employed on a full-time basis preparing the illustrations of previously misinterpreted or completely new species.

However, the more traditional method of depicting orchids in water-colours has by no means died out and the last few years has seen a resurgence of the publication of very large and very expensively produced books on plants containing reproductions of specially commissioned paintings. Margaret Mee's *Flowers of the Brazilian Forests* (Tryon Gallery) contains many orchids and I have been personally involved in writing the text to complement the recently published massive *Orchidaceae* with illustrations by Mary Grierson (Bourton Press) and the *Folio of Orchid Paintings* by James Walford (Medici Society).

Several books have appeared in the last few years dealing solely with the colour photography of natural history subjects such as flowers. As examples of photographed flowers, a quick glance at any of these books shows that orchids are more sought after than any other plants. The colour photography of orchids and the subsequent mass colour printing of the photographs has improved in quality more than anything else involved with orchids. A little more than thirty years ago a book's colour plates derived from photographs were usually poorly printed and most volumes rarely had more than a handful. Today such books as Luer's *The Native Orchids of the United States and Canada* (New York Botanical Garden) and Williamson's *The Orchids of South Central Africa* (Dent), although in the middle price range, both contain literally hundreds of superbly reproduced colour photographs of orchids. Even the more ephemeral magazines on orchids include an ever-increasing number of colour photographs each month.

Bletilla striata, *shown here in an early hand-coloured illustration, is often called* Bletilla *or* Bletia hyacinthina. *This orchid comes from China and, despite its exotic appearance, is sufficiently hardy to flower outdoors in many parts of north-western Europe and North America.*

Orchids for the Amateur Grower

Out of the 18,000 or more wild species of orchid currently accepted and the tens of thousands of hybrids that have been flowered about 6,000 are widely grown. Perhaps it would be wiser to say that the remainder are very difficult to obtain as they are either very rare species or they are hybrids which were never widely propagated and distributed.

The following chapters list the species and hybrids that are fairly widely available or of such particular scientific, historical or decorative value that they should be sought after. It is always useful to have a few of the more unusual plants to bargain with when exchanging!

The list of orchid genera appended to this book lists those genera that have had at least one of their species cultivated with success. Many of them are species from the temperate regions of Europe and North America and can only be cultivated in an 'alpine' house or out of doors. All the genera are arranged according to subtribes because it is usually only within the subtribe that genera will inter-breed, although there are many exceptions.

What orchids can the amateur grow? Many factors have to be taken into account, such as the size of the greenhouse, the heating system, the money available to run the heating system and other automated equipment and to buy the initial stock of plants and, perhaps most important of all, the amount of time available for the essentially manual and non-automated tasks such as removing dead leaves and repotting, and checking the automatic equipment.

Many orchid catalogues offer special collections for the new grower but it is a better idea to go to an orchid nursery and tell the salesman exactly the sort of conditions you can provide and the time you have available. So that the new grower is not overwhelmed with a large collection of plants to look after at one time, many nurserymen operate a 'Plant-a-Month' scheme or even a 'Seedling' or a 'Mericlone' each month. These schemes usually have an added attraction in that they can be paid for on an extended credit purchase basis.

When obtaining your initial collection, it is advisable to have species only, as they will not be superseded by bigger and better plants as always happens with hybrids. Furthermore, the exact cultural requirements of species are very well known, which is more than can be said of many hybrids.

The following list is based on correspondence with the much-lamented David Sander, of Sander's Orchid Nursery fame, who passed away in 1974 and who did so very much to re-popularize orchid growing after the Second World War. All will grow in an intermediate or cool-house provided that temperatures do not fall below 10°C (50°F) at any time. They represent a considerable range of the plant and flower shape and colour-types found in the orchid family and in the author's experience all are tolerant of some degree of neglect but will, nonetheless, respond well if given extra care.

The beginner's twenty

Ada aurantiaca, Cattleya skinneri, Coelogyne cristata, Cymbidium tracyanum, Dendrobium delicatum, Dendrobium nobile, Epidendrum cochleatum, Epidendrum ibaguense, Laelia anceps, Lycaste cruenta, Masdevallia coccinea, Maxillaria picta, Miltonia vexillaria, Odontoglossum crispum, Odontoglossum grande, Oncidium cheirophorum, Osmoglossum pulchellum, Paphiopedilum insigne, Pleione formosana, Zygopetalum Blackii.

Ada aurantiaca *and its variety* punctata, *shown here, is an attractive plant for a first collection of orchids. It is often used in breeding to add orange to* Oncidium – *group hybrids.*

Cattleya group

To those uninitiated to the mystique of orchids and, often, to the orchid enthusiasts themselves, the word 'orchid', despite its etymological derivation, conjures up in the mind a picture of a deep reddish purple *Cattleya* flower. As an illustration on a box of particularly expensive chocolates, a wedding bouquet, a corsage at a coming-out ball or a luxuriantly flowering plant in a darkened greenhouse, the clear lilacs, deep magenta-purples and rich crimsons of Cattleyas are archetypal orchids to many of us.

Cattleyas summarize all the mysteries of orchids; hot humid jungles, daring plant explorers, high prices paid at auctions for rare plants – all are closely associated with Cattleyas. But how true is this picture?

The larger flowered Cattleyas and their associates such as Laelias do come from places such as the hot damp Amazonian rain forests but many species especially from related genera such as *Epidendrum* occur in much drier and cooler localities throughout south and central America and the West Indies. Many tales are related of the first collecting of Cattleyas by the explorers employed by the early European orchid nurserymen; some stories obviously have gained much in the telling but others are true. The discovery and obtaining of the white-flowered form of *Cattleya skinneri* (*C. s.* 'Alba') by Benedikt Roezl in 1870 is an oft-quoted story but is an excellent example of its genre.

Roezl, a collector of considerable repute and whose name is today enshrined in orchid literature in the unusually showy *Pleurothallis roezlii*, was coming to the end of a successful collecting trip in Guatemala. Just one more overnight stay in a coastal village and he could start to load his plants on the ship. Walking along with his heavily laden mule-train, and probably not concentrating very hard on his route now that the days of hard work and hardship were over, he lost his way and was immediately confronted by an armed bandit. Two of the bandit's accomplices barred his retreat and, despite offering them his remaining money, he was taken to their hideout. A local priest had also been captured but was soon released because of his protestations. Roezl tried a

Cattleya mossiae is a Venezuelan species which has been in cultivation since 1836. It is still widely grown and also widely used as a parent.

similar ploy and was soon also released, and the two of them walked to the village together. They conversed very little. Roezl was deep in thought about the fate of his plants and the priest could do nothing but bemoan the fact that his birds, the pride and joy of the village, had all been killed by their opponents at the last cock fight. Despite the apparent lack of amity, the priest invited Roezl to his house next to the church. On the turf roof of the church were many orchid plants growing, there being an Indian custom of planting unusually fine specimens as a devotion on or near their churches. Roezl's interest was suddenly aroused when he saw a white *Flor de San Sebastian* (*Cattleya skinneri* 'Alba') among the other orchids.

Realizing that it would be impossible to buy the plant, Roezl reasoned that the only way to obtain it would be to devise a method of ensuring that the village cocks won their next fight. The technicalities of his method are not recorded but on the following Sunday the priest was delighted that all his birds won their fights. Roezl was rewarded with the white *Cattleya* and it was sent to England at all possible speed where it fetched £300 from an orchid collector from Manchester.

Types available

There are fifty distinct genera comprising about 850 species in the *Cattleya* group (technically called subtribe *Laeliinae*) and a surprisingly large number of them are cultivated wherever orchids are grown. Many of the genera have very few species, usually less than ten; for example, *Caularthron*, *Rhyncholaelia*, *Laeliopsis* and *Domingoa* have two species each, *Jacquiniella* and *Nageliella* have three each and *Alamania*, *Sophronitella*, *Broughtonia* and *Loefgrenianthus* are single specied. Among the larger cultivated genera are *Barkeria* with ten species and *Laelia* with thirty. *Brassavola* and *Hexadesmia* have fifteen each and *Schomburgkia* seventeen. However, it is the largest genera which are more widely grown; *Cattleya* itself has about sixty species, *Encyclia* (often included in *Epidendrum*) has one hundred and thirty and *Epidendrum* well over four hundred.

A great range of plant sizes, and flower colours,

shapes and sizes are found in the *Cattleya* group and, not surprisingly, they were among the first to be hybridized on a large scale by orchid breeders. The first hybrid was *Cattleya* Dominiana, a cross between *C. intermedia* and *maxima*, made by Veitch in 1859, only three years after the first orchid hybrid ever. *Cattleya* group species cross-breed much more readily than many orchids to produce a huge range of intra-generic and inter-generic hybrids.

This ability of Cattleyas to produce hybrids readily extends to the wild where several crosses have been recorded. Two examples still grown today are *Cattleya × guatemalensis* (*Cattleya aurantiaca × skinneri*) and *Cattleya × victoria-regina* (*Cattleya labiata × leopoldii*) and there are even wild intergenerics, such as the well-known *Laeliocattleya elegans* (*Cattleya leopoldii × Laelia purpurata*) from the Brazilian rainforests.

Every orchid grower has his or her likes and dislikes as to size and shape of plants and their flowers, and every orchid house has its failures and successes. It may be thought invidious to provide a list, but below a wide range of well-tried and available plants is suggested for any *Cattleya*-group collection. Trial and error, and finance, will determine what you can grow and there are well over five thousand hybrid grexes and species and untold tens of thousands of cultivars to choose from. Very few species new to science are discovered in the wild except in *Epidendrum* itself but the list of *Cattleya*-group registered hybrids is increasing by at least two hundred and fifty each year constituting a range of plants exceptional in the variety of flower shape and colour.

Suggested plants
Barkeria
skinneri.

Brassavola (including **Rhyncholaelia**)
acaulis, cucullata, digbyana, glauca, inodosa.

Brassocattleya
Déesse, Hartland, Heaven's Sake, Mount Hood, November Bride.

Left and above : Cattleyas (far left and above) were among the orchids that were first grown and hybridized but as they require hot conditions to be maintained in the greenhouse they are not now so popular. C. loddigesii (far left) requires bright conditions to flower freely. Laeliocattleyas (left) are almost unique among intergeneric hybrids in that natural ones are known.

Brassolaeliocattleya
Buttercup, Dinsmore, Gomari, Malworth, Melrose, Norman's Bay, Nugget.

Cattleya
amethystoglossa, bicolor, bowringiana, citrina (=Encyclia citrina), dowiana, forbesii, granulosa, guttata, intermedia, labiata, loddigesii, mossiae, skinneri, trianaei, walkerana, Bob Betts, Bow Bells, Enid, Fabia, Margaret Stewart, Pearl Harbour.

Epidendrum (including Encyclia)
atropurpureum, brassavolae, ciliare, citrina, cochleatum, crassilabium, fragrans, ibaguense, mariae, nemorale, nocturnum, prismatocarpum, pseudepidendrum, radicans, stamfordianum, stenopetalum, wallisii, Brownie.

Laelia
anceps, autumnalis, cinnabarina, harpophylla, milleri, pumila, purpurata, xanthina.

Laeliocattleya
Amber Gold, Ann Follis, Blue Boy, Bonanza, Edgard van Belle, Golden Gate, Lorraine Shirai, Pacific Sun, Princess Margaret, Rosa Kirsch, Twinkle Star.

Potinara
Bunty, Medea, Red Friar, Tapestry Peak.

Schomburgkia
crispa, lyonsii, splendida, tibicinis, undulata.

Sophrolaeliocattleya
Anzac, Canzac, Jewel Box, Lindores, Rainbow Hill, Sunburst.

Sophronitis
coccinea.

Cultivation
Most species and hybrids in the *Cattleya* group require an intermediate or warm house but some of the high altitude Epidendrums, such as *fragrans* and *nemorale*, thrive at lower temperatures. Although full summer sun is not desirable, all plants need fairly high light levels. Most plants have a well-marked seasonal growth pattern where a definite resting phase follows the period of active growth and flowering. Cattleyas and their allies require a damp atmosphere during rapid growth but the resting phase must be drier. Nevertheless more Cattleyas are lost by over-watering and over-humid conditions at the wrong time than by any other mishap. Cattleyas can withstand high temperatures providing the humidity rises accordingly and this means that careful ventilation is often necessary. In all cases winter temperatures must not fall below 10°C (50°F) and for those plants in the warm house ideally a minimum of 14°C (57°F) is necessary. Some shading may be needed, particularly when growths are tender.

Plants in this alliance thrive in relatively small pots and especially useful are those with large air- and drainage-holes in the sides and base; teak or redwood 'log cabin' type baskets are perfect for the larger species of *Cattleya* and for the intergenerics involving those species. The traditional potting medium is two parts osmunda fibre to one part sphagnum moss but, because of the costs and difficulties in supply, a mixture of coarse fir-bark and sphagnum, together with plastic fibres and granules and charcoal, gives excellent results. Frequent feeding is desirable for Cattleyas.

Cattleyas like most orchids can suffer from virus diseases, but healthy plants are seldom troubled. A systemic insecticide is the best cure for the aphids which probably carry the offending virus and is also the only real solution to the common problem of scale attack. In Europe slugs are another pest but good greenhouse hygiene will prevent this.

Propagation
Repotting and dividing the plants should be carried out when it is necessary either to produce another plant or when the compost has decayed or when the plant has obviously outgrown its container. In the commercial nursery meristem culture of desirable cultivars is carried out on an ever-increasing scale and has been responsible for the stabilization of prices for both the common and the more rarely encountered species and hybrids.

Previous page : Brassavola digbyana 'Fimbriata' is much used to produce intergeneric hybrids such as Brassocattleya, Bassolaeliocattleya and Brassolaelia.

Laelia harpophylla, *a Brazilian plant, has a much smaller flower than most* Laelia *species but its colour makes it much sought after as a parent.*

Cymbidium *Dag was first raised in California in 1964, its parents being* Cym. *Esmerelda and* Cym. pumilum.

Cymbidium group

Although the layman probably visualizes a chocolate-box type *Cattleya* flower whenever orchids are mentioned, it is *Cymbidium* species and hybrids that spell out orchids to most growers today.

There are many reasons for the popularity of Cymbidiums but the two main ones are that they require very little heat to survive and that their flowers are very long lasting. In addition, the flowers of most types are arranged along an arching inflorescence and hence are particularly valuable to the cut-flower trade which uses them extensively for bouquets and corsages.

Many of the species of *Cymbidium*, especially those from India, have been cultivated in Europe for a very long time, where their low temperature requirements meant that they would thrive and flower successfully in a conservatory. However, many centuries before this, the Japanese grew Cymbidiums not for their flowers, which in the case of many Japanese species are not very colourful and often borne singly, but for the beauty of their leaves. These leaves apparently were often variegated in alternating stripes of cream and green, but we now believe this to be a result of virus infection.

Cymbidiums are also well worth trying for the tyro orchid grower, as they do not require a very specialized medium, doing well in peat and plastic mixtures as well as very fibrous loam.

Another factor in the ever-increasing popularity of Cymbidiums is that they respond very readily to meristem culture and, as a consequence, many types are much cheaper than species or hybrids of other groups. The very newest hybrids can command very high prices of several hundred each but this is still relatively cheap, when the longevity and ease of cultivation of the plants and the longevity and abundance of the flowers are considered.

Types available

Although there are six genera currently listed as belonging to the subtribe *Cymbidiinae*, only four are usually represented in collections, the two rare ones *Dipodium* and *Porphyroglottis* being difficult to grow.

By far the most common genus is *Cymbidium* itself with over forty species distributed throughout South-East Asia, the Pacific Islands and the tropical regions of Australia. *Grammatophyllum* is dealt with in the chapter on Asiatic orchids and the two African representatives, *Cymbidiella* and *Grammangis*, in the chapter on African orchids.

Most of the forty *Cymbidium* species have been grown at some time or other but it is the multiple-flowered types that are the most popular. However, today, none of the species are widespread in collec-

tions, as it is the countless man-made hybrids that are listed surprisingly cheaply in almost every commercial nurseryman's catalogue.

The first hybrid in the genus was flowered in 1889 and was between the two popular species *C. eburneum* and *C. lowianum* which the raiser at Veitch's nursery called *C.* Eburneo-Lowianum. This was an instant success but very little other hybridizing was carried out in the genus until Mr. H. G. Alexander, the orchid grower at Lt. Col. Sir George Holford's Westonbirt house, crossed the Veitch plant with the

pale rosy-red flowered *C. insigne*. The resulting progeny were to become probably the most famous orchids in the world and their name *Cymbidium* Alexanderi a household name to all orchid growers. The best form was selected by Mr. Alexander and called 'Westonbirt'. Ever since the debut of this plant in 1911 it has been repeatedly used as a parent along with the other species usually used such as *giganteum*, *erythrostylum*, *grandiflorum* and *tracyanum*.

Because of chromosome disturbances, some of them man-induced, during the reproductive processes, and by carefully selecting only the largest flowered plants as parents, the average size of the flowers of *Cymbidium* hybrids today is very much bigger than any of the species. The range of colours available, from purest unspotted whites, yellows and greens to deep chocolatey-maroons, crimsons and pinks and any combination of these, is much greater than in any other group of orchids. It is remarkable that so many different forms, each one only differing very slightly from the next but all of a unique quality, should have been derived from basically so very few parent species. *Cymbidium* hybrids are still entering the monthly list of newly registered hybrids at a rate which shows no signs of slowing down.

Suggested plants
Cymbidium

aloifolium, atropurpureum, bicolor, canaliculatum, chloranthum, dayanum, devonianum, eburneum, elegans, ensifolium, erythrostylum, faberi, finlaysonianum, giganteum, gracillimum, grandiflorum, insigne, kanran, lancifolium, lowianum, madidum, mastersii, niveomarginatum, pendulum, pubescens, pumilum, simulans, sinense, suave, suavissimum, tigrinum, tracyanum, virescens, Alexanderi, Babylon, Balkis, Baltic, Cambria, Dag, Dorama, Fred Stewart, King Arthur, Mary Ann, Miretta, Pearl-

Opposite: Cymbidium Plover 'Fuchsia' is a hybrid raised by the British breeder Mr Alexander; the parents are Cym. *Lowiograndiflorum* and Cym. *Pauwelsii*.

Above: the name Cymbidium *is derived from the Greek 'kymbe', a boat, referring to the boat-shaped hollow of the lip; this characteristic is sometimes obscured in hybrids.*

Balkis, Plover, San Miguel, Showgirl, Stanley Fouraker, Sussex Down, Vieux Rose.

Cultivation

It has been reported by many growers that the air temperature of their *Cymbidium* house often falls to within a degree of freezing and this has no effect on their plants. Nevertheless it is better to regard 7°C (45°F) as the average minimum for mature plants: young seedlings and newly-purchased mericlones should not really be allowed to fall much below 16°C (60°F). To encourage the development of the inflorescences, summer temperatures must not be allowed to rise too high, and shading the house from direct sunlight even in March and April is frequently necessary. However, autumn sun is to be encouraged, as it rarely produces such high 'in-house' temperatures as spring sun and, in any case, the plants must be fully ripened before the flowering season commences.

The growing medium can be a mixture of any fibrous material such as osmunda or polypodium or tree fern, peat, sphagnum moss, fibrous loam and plastic shreddings. Fir bark and shredded oak and beech leaves have been used by some growers with considerable success, but in all cases it must be remembered that Cymbidiums are rather more greedy than many orchids and the addition of a slow release fertilizer, such as bone meal, is essential.

Foliar feeding of Cymbidiums is a useful technique for maintaining the health of vigorously growing plants but excessive feeding must be avoided as this encourages virus disease to manifest itself.

Growers of Cymbidiums in the southern hemisphere, and South Africa, Australia and New Zealand, all of which have a well-developed *Cymbidium* industry embracing both growing and breeding, should refer to orchid growing manuals written specially for those countries.

Propagation

Cymbidiums are very amenable to all the ways in which orchids can be multiplied. The amateur grower will find that by removing the 'back bulbs', older pseudobulbs with eye shoots, and re-potting them the average greenhouse will soon be over flowing with plants to exchange. However, to enable more plants to be grown in a given space, it is perfectly possible to grow orchids in a bed in the greenhouse, which obviates the wasteful spaces between pots when the plants are grown in the normal way.

Opposite : Cymbidium *Showgirl (* Cym. *Alexanderi × * Cym. *Sweetheart) is one of the many successful hybrids raised from the Alexanderi grex.*

Above : two contrasting examples of Cymbidium *hybrids. That on the left is* Cym. Cambria *(* Cym.

Carisbrook × Cym. *Ramboda), raised in 1948, while that on the right is an unnamed early hybrid.*

Dendrobium group

My personal favourites among all commonly cultivated orchids are Dendrobiums. The genus is the
largest in the orchid family with over 1,400 species
occurring from the Himalayas to the Pacific Islands
with many species also to be found in Australia.

In the subtribe *Dendrobiinae* there are several other
genera which can be cultivated but none are anything
as large as *Dendrobium* and none have the range of
flower colours and forms exhibited by that genus.
Species of *Ephemerantha* and *Diplocaulobium* produce
flowers of great delicacy but they usually last for only
a day or even only a few hours. The genus *Eria* is of
great interest botanically and its flowers have a great
range of form and colour but all except a few are very
small flowered and most are difficult to obtain.
Porpax is a very odd genus with only ten species,
some of which have flattened pseudobulbs from which
the small flowers arise directly when the plant is
leafless.

Most Dendrobiums have reed-like stems, which
are usually termed 'pseudobulbs' but only a few
species have really typically bulbous ones. The leaves
are arranged in two rows along the stems and vary
greatly in shape and shades of green. Flowers can be
borne singly or in globose or elongated inflorescences
either at the top of the flowering stem or laterally at
intervals along its length.

Dendrobiums are either evergreen or deciduous,
the former coming mainly from the hot humid
tropical rain forests of Borneo, New Guinea and
adjoining islands and the latter from the more
seasonally fluctuating climatic regimes of mainland
Asia. All are epiphytic, some forming great clumps in
the crotch of a tree and others dangling down from
the lower branches of trees and shrubs.

An odd phenomenon is exhibited by the common
Malayan species *Dendrobium crumenatum* and several
of its relatives in that nearly all the plants in one area
flower at the same time. For many years the reason for
this was not understood but it is now thought to be a
response to a low temperature a few days beforehand.

As well as a great range of colours, *Dendrobium*
flowers are frequently ornamented by incisions and

Dendrobium heterocarpum
(*commonly called* Den.
aureum) *is a widely
cultivated eastern Asiatic
orchid.*

lacinations of the lip margins, which in *D. brymeranum* and its allies give it the appearance of being encrusted with exotic lichens.

Dendrobium flowers are characterized in many species by their longevity which, in cultivation in the unpollinated state, can be up to nine months. However, as soon as pollination occurs, the flowers wither very quickly.

Mention must also be made of the scents produced by most *Dendrobium* flowers. They are neither so excessively sweet as those of Cattleyas nor so disgustingly rich as those of many Bulbophyllums, being pervasive yet not overpowering.

Types available

It would be invidious to select certain Dendrobiums as being particularly desirable but some advice is offered in an attempt to render a final choice from the

1,400 species and thousands of hybrids less daunting. A point to remember is that the deciduous species, and hybrids derived from them, require less heat and a well defined resting phase, and the evergreen species and hybrids a continuous period at a higher temperature. The two groups cannot usually be grown together to full flowering perfection in the same house, and this can restrict the choice. The beginner is well advised to concentrate on the Indian species (cool, deciduous), such as *Dendrobium nobile*, *primulinum*, *pierardii* (or *aphyllum* as it is called), *aggregatum*, *wardianum*, and *farmeri* and the many hybrids that have been produced especially recently by Japanese hybridists.

Once these 'easy' species and hybrids have been mastered, the evergreens should be attempted. The so-called 'antelope' types, characterized by their long, erect spirally twisted antelope-horn like petals are

Above: Dendrobium spectabile *is a native of New Guinea and adjacent Pacific islands but it is threatened in its natural habitat as a result of over-collecting.*

Opposite: Dendrobium Anne Marie *(Den. Montrose × Den. Winifred Fortescue) was raised in 1963 by Wichmann Orchids of Celle, West Germany.*

Overleaf: the Burmese species Dendrobium infundibulum *is found at high altitudes; it was first introduced into cultivation in 1858.*

Dendrobium delicatum *is found in New South Wales and Queensland, Australia. Some authorities consider this orchid a true species while others believe it is a naturally occuring hybrid.*

particularly desirable as hybridization has produced a wide range of colours and it is here that the longest-lived flowers, such as those of *D. stratiotes*, are found. As well as this kind, there are the '*D. bigibbum*' type, so called because this particular species is very well known as it is the state flower of Queensland. The flower colour of this species and its close relatives is deep rich pink and pinkish-maroon and, in hybridization, this has been transmitted to a greater or lesser extent to a great number of plants.

Suggested plants
Dendrobium

aggregatum, arachnites, atroviolaceum, aureum, bellatulum, bigibbum, brymeranum, canaliculatum, chrysotoxum, crassinode, crepidatum, cruentum, crystallinum, cucumerinum, dearei, delacourii, delicatum, denneanum, dixanthum, falconeri, fimbriatum, formosum, gouldii, gracilicaule, hercoglossum, infundibulum, johnsoniae, kingianum, lituiflorum, lowii, macarthiae, macrophyllum, moniliforme, moschatum, nobile, papilio, parishii, phalaenopsis, pierardii, primulinum, pulchellum, regale, regium, sanderae, sanguinolentum, schulleri, schutzei, senile, speciosum, speciosissimum, spectabile, stratiotes, strebloceras, superbiens, superbum, taurinum, thrysiflorum, toftii, tokai, undulatum, veratrifolium, victoria-reginae, wardianum, williamsianum, Akatuke, Alice Chong, Anne Marie, Bali, Evening Glow, Gatton Monarch, Helen Park, Louis Bleriot, May Neal, Orion, Thwaitesiae.

Cultivation

The two types of *Dendrobium* species and hybrids, deciduous and evergreen, require quite different conditions from each other and it is not desirable to put them together in a single *Dendrobium* house.

The deciduous types require a cool resting phase but the evergreens need consistently higher temperatures. Adequate light is required by all plants but it is especially important with the evergreen types that originally come from the high-light tropical regions. If a plant accidentally dries out, the best way to deal with it is to dip the pot into water to thoroughly soak the potting compost.

Dendrobiums will thrive on any standard epiphytic orchid compost but to ensure that the plants flower well they must never be overpotted. A plant with its roots dangling over the edge of the pot is much more likely to flower than one with its roots having ample room to spread within the pot.

Propagation

Dendrobiums can be divided in the traditional way but with most species the quickest way to multiply stocks is to remove and pot the little plantlets that are found on nearly all mature plants.

Dendrobium thyrsiflorum *is a particularly attractive species from Burma. Though known throughout the orchid world by this name it should properly be called variety* albolutea *of* Den. densiflorum.

Paphiopedilum group

The lady's slipper orchids are quite different in their appearance from most other orchids because the labellum is always expanded into an oddly shaped pouched slipper or shoe. Technically there are other differences connected with the detailed structure of the column and several eminent taxonomists have suggested that they should be placed into a family separate from the rest of the orchids. The tendency today is not to distinguish them as the *Cypripediaceae* but, nevertheless, to treat them as a very distinct sub family of the *Orchidaceae*.

Five genera are distinguishable in the sub-family *Cypripedioideae*: *Cypripedium*, *Paphiopedilum*, *Phragmipedium*, *Selenipedium* and *Criosanthes*. The first occurs throughout the temperate regions of the northern hemisphere, where its fifty plus species are widely grown as garden plants. As a consequence of their horticultural appeal and the fact that many grow in vulnerable habitats, many Cypripediums are becoming rare. In England *C. calceolus* is known in the wild from only two plants but it is quite common in gardens. *Criosanthes* is a single-specied genus occurring in China and North America.

Phragmipedium and *Selenipedium* both occur in tropical America where they form large clumps of leaves through which the large flower-spikes thrust themselves. Several species are cultivated but especially attractive are some of the *Phragmipedium* species which have flowers with excessively long thin petals that dangle down where they possibly act as an attractive device for pollinating insects.

The genus that is most widely cultivated is *Paphiopedilum* where the fifty plus species have now been joined by many thousands of hybrids raised by man. Personally, I feel that the almost spherical and obscenely glistening flowers of many of the modern hybrids should not be classified as orchids as they have lost the essentially natural orchid-flower appearance of three sepals, two petals and a labellum all distinct from each other. However, this is very much a personal view and at the same time I must feel great admiration for the hybridists who have produced such a range of flower colours in such a short period.

Paphiopedilum sukhakulii, *a recently discovered species native to Thailand, is closely related to* Paph. wardii.

Very recently, as a result of many collecting expeditions into the more remote corners of South-East Asia in such countries as Indonesia, Thailand and the Philippines, several distinct Paphiopedilums have appeared on the market. Although not really warranting recognition as botanically distinct species, they have re-awakened the interest in more natural looking Paphiopedilums and their special characteristics have led to their being in great demand as parents for more hybrids.

The commoner species of *Paphiopedilum*, such as *insigne*, *tonsum* and *venustum*, and early hybrids such as *P.* Maudiae are cheap to purchase, but the rarer species, such as *rothschildianum* and *stonei* and the most recently introduced hybrids often fetch surprisingly high prices. *Paphiopedilum* species have always been in considerable demand because of the relative ease with which they can be persuaded to produce their bizarre flowers in cultivation. The demand was such in the middle years of the last century that orchid nurseries and their paid collectors would take great pains not only to refuse information on the whereabouts of plants but in some cases to give quite erroneous data that would ensure that no competitors could collect all the plants first.

John Whitehead, the collector, found the rare *P.*

rothschildianum on the slopes of Mt. Kinabalu in Borneo, but when Messrs. Linden, the famous Belgian orchid firm, introduced the plant to the market, it was called *Cypripedium neoguineense*! The *Cypripedium* part of the name was correct at that time (1857) but *neoguineense* indicated that it came from New Guinea and not Borneo. The issuing of erroneous information on an orchid's provenance still continues today and rarely is it due to a genuine error!

Types Available

All species of *Paphiopedilum* are worth a place in any orchid collection but it must be remembered that there are two main groups within the genus, each of which requires quite distinct conditions. The entirely green-leaved species come from the cooler and usually more mountainous parts of Asia but the mottled and tessellated two-tone types require much more heat.

If there is room for only a few plants, it is suggested that consideration should be given to the multi-flowered species, such as *haynaldianum* and *lowii*, which are usually neglected in favour of the single-flowered species and their hybrid derivatives. Also desirable are the predominantly white-flowered species found in the Malayan Peninsula; perhaps the pale mauve-flushed *P. delenatii*.

Above: Paphiopedilum bellatulum *(left) is a tessellated-leaved species from Thailand and*

Indonesia. Paphiopedilum concolor *(right) is a very variable species from Thailand.*

Opposite: Paphiopedilum victoria-regina *subspecies* glaucophyllum *is a widely grown and frequently hybridized Asiatic species.*

Suggested plants
Paphiopedilum

acmodontum, appletonianum, argus, barbatum, bellatulum, bougainvilleanum, boxallii, bullenianum, callosum, chamberlainianum, charlesworthii, concolor, curtisii, dayanum, delenatii, fairieanum, glauco-phyllum, godefroyae, haynaldianum, hookerae, insigne, javanicum, lawrenceanum, linii, lowii, mastersianum, niveum, parishii, philippinense, primulinum, purpuratum, robinsonii, rothschildianum, spiceranum, stonei, sukhakulii, venustum, victoria-regina, villosum, volonteanum, Amanda, Baroque, Blackburn, Blagrose, Botan, Cadense, Dusty Miller, F. C. Puddle, Floramond, Geelong, Hellas, Lemon Hart, Maudiae, Paeony, Small World, Transvaal, Winston Churchill.

Phragmipedium

boissieranum, caricinum, caudatum, klotzschianum, lindleyanum, longifolium, sargentianum, schlimii, vittatum, Grande, Praying Mantis, Sedenii.

Cultivation

Paphiopedilums and their relatives are non-pseudo-bulbous plants and hence do not have the water storage and drought resistance found in many other groups. Therefore, a major requirement of their successful cultivation is an ample supply of water, although equally damaging to a plant is an incorrectly potted and badly drained growing medium.

The tessellated and plain green-leaved forms require different temperature regimes, but most can be accommodated in a single greenhouse provided that the temperature never falls below 15°C (60°F) and that adequate shading is given in summer.

The potting medium can be of the traditional natural fibre type but it is always worth experimenting with the addition of plastic shreds or granules. If available, a higher proportion, up to 60%, of the mixture can be chopped sphagnum moss. Some types do well in a plastic and sphagnum mixture.

Propagation

Paphiopedilums are very difficult to propagate by meristem culture but all other methods are readily applied.

Paphiopedilum *Hellas was first raised by the British orchid breeder Mr Alexander in 1940, the parents being* Paph. Desdemona *and* Paph. Tannia. *It has itself now been used as a parent.*

Vanda group

The 'Vandaceous' orchids comprise just over 900 species scattered throughout tropical Asia, tropical and sub-tropical Australia and the Pacific Islands. There are 75 genera but many of these have only one or very few species each and, in most cases, the flowers are very small and insignificant. Of the largest genera three rarely have representative species grown in greenhouses (*Thrixspermum*: 100 species, *Sarcanthus*: 100 species, *Taeniophyllum*: 120 species) but *Phalaenopsis* (35 species), *Aërides* (40 species) and *Vanda* (60 species) are among the most popular of all orchids grown anywhere in the world.

To these species have been added many thousands of hybrids between species in the same genus and species of different genera. The number of registered hybrid genera is growing at a rapid rate as the results of past crossings come into flower. Almost every major genus has been crossed with every other genus, and the results of these crossed with each other and so on, so that there are now over 120 hybrid genera in existence. The pioneer hybridization programmes were carried out by the Singapore Botanic Gardens over fifty years ago but the very first hybrids, in *Vanda*, were made about eighty years ago.

Nevertheless, it is the species that still have great popularity as decorative plants, being grown not only in greenhouses in the temperate world but as garden plants in their areas of origin. Most plants in the *Vanda* group are what are called 'monopodial' in their growth habit. The technical nature of this is not relevant to orchid growing but the practicality of it is that by and large monopodial orchids have an upright habit and usually require some support if grown in a greenhouse or open garden bed. The stem continues to grow in length and the leaves are interspersed with roots and inflorescences so that the resulting plant is quite different from most other orchids.

Phalaenopsis plants and their relatives are exceptions to this and are usually tufted plants, but the flower spikes occasionally produce little plantlets which can be potted and eventually removed. *Phalaenopsis* plants are also exceptional in that the most strikingly beautiful flowers are almost wholly pure white. *P. amabilis*,

Phalaenopsis *Ruby Zada* (Phal. *Zada* × Phal. *Ruby Lips*) *has proved one of the most successful of all* Phalaenopsis *hybrids. It was first raised in 1965.*

Above : Phalaenopsis
*Freed's Angel. (*Phal. *Show
Girl* × Phal. *Ruby Zada*)
*was raised in 1975 in
California.*

Opposite : Ascocenda
*Mangkiatkul (*Vanda
Jennie Hashimoto ×
Ascocenda *Meda Arnold),*
*a product of breeding
programmes in Thailand,
was first raised in 1968.*

the moth orchid in many languages, has, arguably, the most beautiful flowers of any orchid, with its very large wing-like petals, slightly smaller sepals and quite small yellow and scarlet marked labellum. *P. sanderana* is similar in shape but the tepals are distinctly red or mauve striped. By crossing *Phalaenopsis* plants with *Doritis pulcherrima*, the resulting *Doritaenopsis* hybrids exhibit a great range of colours especially in the labellum, which can be a deep velvety crimson.

However, it is *Vanda* species and their hybrids that epitomize orchids from South-East Asia. They have been known for a very long time and many stories are told of their collection and importation into Europe.

The German collector, Roeblen, who was employed for many years by Sander's orchid establishment, had incredible adventures in Mindanao, one of the Philippines group, in his search for *Vanda sanderana*. It was in 1880 that he first went there to collect orchids for Sander and almost immediately was unwittingly caught up in the struggles between the colonizing Spaniards and the native inhabitants. Some time later Roeblen was allowed to enter the interior to look for orchid plants but as soon as he reached a likely looking area an earthquake occurred and completely destroyed the village in which he was resting. However, on scrambling out of his ruined native hut he looked up through a hole torn in the roof and saw an orchid quite

Above : Phalaenopsis *Painted Desert is a hybrid dating from* **1966** *between* Phal. *Mrs. J. H. Veitch and* Phal. *Juanita.*

Opposite : Rhynchostylis gigantea '*Illustris*' *comes from South-East Asia and goes by the common name fox-tail orchid.*

unknown to him. After many more privations eventually plants of this new species, soon to be described as *Vanda sanderana*, reached Europe.

V. sanderana is available today at about £30 per plant but as so many plants have been removed by commercial collectors from the wild and because so much of the 'wild' has been destroyed by forest clearance, they have all been raised from seed. It is very well worth growing but its greatest value is as a parent in such world-famous hybrids as *V.* Rothschildiana (*V. coerulea* × *sanderana*).

Types available
It is impossible to really do more than list the species most worthy of attention and those hybrids that have proven themselves over the years. The best advice is to obtain catalogues and visit commercial orchid nurseries so that the plants can be seen in flower. There are so many intergeneric hybrids that it is not really fair to select any one hybrid genus as being better than any other. However, personally, I feel that many growers, if they have not done so already, should try some of the newer grexes of *Ascocenda* (*Ascocentrum* × *Vanda*) not just for the undoubted beauty of their flowers but because the compact nature of the plant and the length of the flowering season, which can be almost continuous, makes them particularly valuable to those with only a limited space.

Suggested plants
Acampe
longifolia.

Aëridachnis
Bogor.

Aërides
crassifolia, falcata, fieldingii, flabellata, japonica, jarckiana, lawrenceae, mitrata, multiflora, odorata.

Aëridovanda
Blue Chips, Suebsanguan.

Arachnis
cathcartii, flos-aëris, hookerana, Ishbel, Maggie Oei.

Aranda
Lily Chong, Lucy Laycock.

Aranthera
Lilliput.

Ascocenda
Blue Boy, Eileen Beauty, Erika Reuter, Mangkiat-kul, Meda Arnold, Medasand, Ophelia, Red Gem, Tan Chai Beng, Yip Sum Wah.

Ascocentrum
ampullaceum, aurantiacum, curvifolium, miniatum, Sagarik Gold.

Christieara
Malibu Gold.

Doritaenopsis
Memoria Clarence Schubert, Red Coral, Red Lip.

Doritis
pulcherrima.

Holttumara
Cochineal.

Luisia
teretifolia.

Phalaenopsis mannii, *an Indian and Vietnamese species, has been much used in breeding.*

Neofinetia
falcata.

Phalaenopsis
amabilis, amboinensis, cochlearis, corningiana, cornu-cervi, denevei, equestris, fasciata, fimbriata, fuscata, gigantea, laycockii, lindenii, leuddemanniana, mannii, mariae, micholtzii, parishii, sanderana, schillerana, serpentilingua, stuartiana, sumatrana, Alice Gloria, Ann Marie Beard, Bruce Shaffer, Doris, Dos Pueblos, Ella Freed, Freed's Angel, Keith Shaffer, Lipperose, Lippezauber, Mad Lips, Miami Maid, Mistinguett, Painted Desert, Peppermint Stick, Ramona, Redfan, Ruby Zada, Show Girl.

Renades
Red Jewel.

Renantanda
Gold Nugget, Violet.

Renanthera
coccinea, histrionica, imschootiana, mututina, *monachica, philippensis, storei,* Brookei Chandler.

Renanthopsis
Apricot Gold, Dana.

Rhynchostylis
coelestis, gigantea, retusa.

Rhynchovanda
Blue Angel, Sagarik Wine.

Sarcochilus
australis, ceciliae, falcatus, hartmannii, hillii.

Trichoglottis
brachiata, fasciata.

Vanda
brunnea, coerulea, coerulescens, cristata, dearei, denisoniana, insignis, lamellata, sanderana, spathulata, teres, tessellata, tricolor, Bill Sutton, Diana Ogawa, Eisensander, Hilo Blue, Jennie Hashimoto, Memoria Madame Pranerm, Onomea,

Vanda coerulea *is the most sought after blue-flowered orchid, being grown for its own merits as a potted plant and as a parent .*

Rothschildiana, Thananchai.

Vandopsis
gigantea, lissochiloides, parishii.

Vascostylis
Blue Fairy.

Cultivation
Nearly all 'Vandaceous' orchids require warm or 'stove' house conditions, although some of the smaller-flowered species from mountainous regions are better when grown in a cooler place. Vandas

require more light than most orchids.

Any of the standard fibrous potting mixtures can be used but many of the group grow and flower equally well or sometimes much better when grown in hanging lath baskets or on rafts of compressed fibre.

Propagation
The long-stemmed types can be chopped in lengths and, provided there are roots and leaves on each length, these will form new plants. Small plantlets can arise on many of the species and hybrids and can be removed and potted. Seed and meristem culture are also widely practised in this group.

Phalaenopsis *Lois Jansen, a cross between* Phal. *Barbara Beard and* Phl. *Ruby Lips, has itself been crossed with* Doritaenopsis *hybrids to give several spectacular plants.*

Odontoglossum group

Tropical America has produced two major types of commonly cultivated orchids, the *Cattleya* and the *Odontoglossum* groups. They are quite distinct in appearance and in their cultural requirements but they are similar in that in each case there are several distinct genera involved and many intra- and inter-generic hybrids have been produced.

The orchids that invariably reached the highest prices in the auction rooms of Europe in the hey-day of orchid importation in the last century were always from one or other of these two groups. *Odontoglossum crispum* was introduced in vast quantities into Britain and it has been recorded that in one occasion over a million plants of this species were unloaded from a single shipment. How many survived the journey to be sold and then grown is not recorded, but collecting on this scale has greatly depleted wild stocks.

Very similar in their general floral shape to Odonto-glossums are most of the species of the genus *Oncidium*. The flowers are of a unique combination of shining chestnut brown and canary yellow and often these are borne on long and straggling inflorescences of up to 2m (6-7ft) or more in length and branched so that a single plant can hold several hundred flowers all out in bloom at one time.

As a marked contrast to these genera, the Miltonias have quite un-orchid-like flowers, very flat and two-dimensional and usually referred to as Pansy orchids. However, the deep velvet maroons, brilliant pinks and whites and combinations of these have made Miltonias one of the most hybridized of all orchids. Their particular features have not been restricted to them-selves and *Miltonia* 'blood' is found in many hybrid genera such as the quinquegeneric *Goodaleara*, *Vuylstekeara* (*Miltonia* × *Cochlioda* × *Odonto-glossum*), and *Charlesworthara* (*Miltonia* × *Cochlioda* × *Oncidium*). These latter two are among the earliest of hybrids involving more than three genera and both are still among the most popular of all orchids. If I was asked to select one grex as summing up the virtues of all intergeneric hybrids and exemplifying man's mastery over nature, *Vuylstekeara* Cambria and especially its cultivar 'Plush' would be my choice.

Odontonia *Eva* (Odontonia *Bleu-ardent* ×
Odontoglossum crispum) *was raised by the British nursery Charlesworth's in 1930.*

Types Available

The list below gives all the important genera, species and hybrids to date but is of necessity a personal listing and nurserymen's catalogues should be consulted to ascertain the latest additions to the ever-growing list of hybrids in this group, which is popular with a large number of orchid growers.

An amateur's collection should always include at the very least one *Odontoglossum* (e.g. *O. crispum, grande, pescatorei*), one *Oncidium* (e.g. *O. cheirophorum, ornithorrhynchum, sphacelatum, varicosum*), one *Miltonia* (e.g. *M. vexillaria, roezlii*) and two or three hybrid generic grexes in *Charlesworthara, Odontocidium* and *Vuylestekeara. Ada aurantiaca* is an unusual orange flowered plant but is well worth getting especially if it is grown alongside its spotted variety (var. *punctata*).

Suggested plants

Ada
aurantiaca.

Aspasia
epidendroides, lunata, principissa, variegata.

Brassia
caudata, gireoudiana, lawrenceana, longissima, maculata, verrucosa.

Charlesworthara
Alpha, Vulcan.

Cochlioda
noezliana, sanguinea.

Ionopsis
utricularioides.

Lockhartia
elegans, lunifera.

Miltonia
candida, clowesii, flavescens, phalaenopsis, regnellii, roezlii, schroederana, spectabilis, vexillaria, warscewiczii, Aurora.

Odontioda
Aloette, Connosa, Elpheon, Florence Stirling, Lautrix.

Opposite : Oncidium *Ella* (Onc. *Mantinii* × O. varicosum*) was raised by Vacherat and Lecoufle in France in 1966.*

Above right : Odontoglossum *Edalva* (Odm. *Edwarcus* × Odm. *Alvarloo) was first made by Charlesworth's in 1959 ; this grex has been used as the basis of further hybrids.*

Above left : Odontoglossum *Royal Serenade (* Odm. *Amphion* × Odm. *Dauphin) is a popular hybrid, which was first registered in 1953.*

Odontocidium
Crowborough, Hebe, Selsfield Gold, Tiger Butter.

Odontoglossum
bictoniense, cervantesii, crispum, grande, halli, harryanum, pendulum, pescatorei, pulchellum, rossii, triumphans, uroskinneri, Edalva, Royal Serenade.

Odontonia
Debutante, Eva, Olga, Santos, Zizette.

Oncidium
altissimum, barbatum, bicallosum, cavendishianum, carthagenense, cheirophorum, concolor, crispum, desertorum, flexuosum, forbesii, harrisonianum, incurvum, jonesianum, krameranum, lanceanum, macranthum, marshallianum, ornithorrhynchum, splendidum, superbiens, tigrinum, triquetrum, varicosum, variegatum, volvox, wentworthianum, Ella.

Rodriguezia
secunda, venusta.

Vuylstekeara
Cambria, Estella Jewel, Insignis, Princess Kaiulani.

Wilsonara
Autumn, Insignis, Jean du Pont, Lyoth, Tangerine, Wendy.

Cultivation
With the exception of Miltonias and some of their hybrid derivatives the *Odontoglossum* group require cool or intermediate house conditions and hence are deservedly popular in these energy-conscious times. Miltonias require slightly higher temperatures but can be grown alongside their congeners provided the minimum winter temperature never falls below 13°C (55°F).

Normal potting media such as fir bark are suitable. Ample water is necessary when plants are actively growing but a dry resting phase is necessary with most plants although the pseudobulbs must never be allowed to shrivel excessively. Light is an important factor and although most plants are tolerant of heavy shade, plenty of light will give much healthier plants provided the air temperature does not rise too high.

Propagation
The usual methods (pages 58–61) are all applicable to members of the group but ordinary division is particularly successful with most plants.

Previous page :
Vuylstekeara *Cambria is a*
trigeneric hybrid. Its
immediate parents were
Vuylstekeara *Rubra and*
Odontoglossum *Clonius.*

Opposite : Miltonia
phalaenopsis *is a*
Colombian species with
grass-like leaves.

Above : Odontoglossum
cervantesii *is a miniature*
species with relatively large
flowers and is a native of
Mexico.

American orchids

The Cattleyas and Odontoglossums and their relatives are deservedly the most popular of all American orchids but there are several other groups which are well worth growing in even the smallest greenhouse. Two of them, *Maxillaria picta* and *Masdevallia coccinea*, are included in the beginner's dozen but many more are equally desirable on account of their flowers and ease of cultivation.

American orchids occur throughout the continent and grow in all climatic regions, but those mostly cultivated today either come from the lowland forests of Brazil, Ecuador, Colombia, Venezuela and central America and the West Indies, or from the middle slopes of the Andes. Thus the first group require mainly stove or warm house conditions but the higher altitude plants can be grown much cooler. Most are epiphytes but there are some spectacular terrestrials such as *Cyrtopodium* species.

Some of the oddest orchids of all are found in America and good examples are found in the widespread genus *Stanhopea*. The inflorescences bearing up to six waxy flowers arise from the base of the pseudobulb and as they are pendulous it is advisable to grow Stanhopeas in hanging pots or baskets from which the flowers can hang down. The flowers themselves produce a very sickly and pungent odour, and there are so many processes developed on the floral parts, and they are arranged in such a seemingly chaotic juxtaposition, that it is difficult to recognize them as orchids.

A near relative is *Catasetum* and its main claim to mention is that, unlike all other orchids, the flowers are either wholly male or wholly female, and so different in appearance that botanists first classified them as belonging to different genera. Whether a plant produces male or female flowers appears to depend on nutritional factors but much more research is necessary to elucidate this strange situation. Catasetums are also unusual in that the pollinia of the male flowers are arranged in the flower in such a way that when they are disturbed they shoot out of the flower for up to 1m (3ft). The purpose of this projectile pollinia is to make sure the pollinating

Zygopetalum *Blackii, an orchid growing well in the intermediate house, is a hybrid involving Z.* crinitum, intermedium *and* maxillare.

insect is frightened away from that flower and goes to another thus ensuring cross-fertilization.

Another oddity among American orchids is the genus *Zygopetalum*. Plants of several species of this have been crossed with other species but the resulting plants are nearly always like the *Zygopetalum* parent whereas in most orchids the hybrids are generally intermediate.

Suggested plants

Acineta
barkeri, chrysantha, superba.

Anguloa
clowesii, uniflora.

Angulocaste
Apollo.

Bifrenaria
harrisoniae.

Catasetum
cernuum, fimbriatum, macrocarpum.

Chondrorhyncha
discolor.

Chysis
aurea, bractescens.

Comparettia
falcata.

Coryanthes
macrantha.

Cycnoches
chlorochilon, dianae, egertonianum, ventricosum.

Eriopsis
biloba.

Gongora
galeata, quinquenervis.

Huntleya
lucida, meleagris.

Leptotes
bicolor.

Lycaste
aromatica, cruenta, lanipes, lawrenceana, macrophylla, skinneri, Auburn.

Masdevallia
bella, chimaera, coccinea, tovarensis.

Maxillaria
grandiflora, luteo-alba, picta, sanderana, striata, venusta.

Mormodes
colossus.

Peristeria
elata.

Pescatorea
cerina.

Pleurothallis
grandis, grobyi, ornata, pectinata, roezlii, stenopetala.

Promenaea
stapelioides, xanthina.

Sobralia
macrantha, xantholeuca.

Stanhopea
grandiflora, oculata, tigrina.

Zygopetalum
crinitum, mackayi, maxillare, Blackii.

Cultivation and Propagation
This depends entirely on the particular plants and no generalizations can be made as these plants come from a wide range of habitats. Specialist textbooks should be consulted.

The striking shape of the tropical South American Anguloa uniflora *has earned it the name of tulip orchid.*

African orchids

Africa is a vast continent with many widely differing climatic and vegetational regions. Orchids are found throughout Africa and their flowers are equally widely different in their sizes, shapes and colours. Nevertheless Africa is nothing like so rich in orchids as South America or Asia, both New Guinea and Colombia for example having more than the whole of the African continent.

Many African orchids are terrestrials especially in the sparsely forested plains and savannah-like areas of eastern Africa. The genera *Disa*, *Habenaria*, *Satyrium* and *Eulophia* are widespread and in many ways their species resemble temperate ones in that they often bear tall upright spikes of reddish or white flowers, and can colonize very large areas of marshland and grassland.

The western side of Africa is more thickly covered with forest than the east and consequently there are many epiphytic species to be found. Zaire and the aptly named Impenetrable Forest of the Ugandan-Zaire border are particularly rich in epiphytes such as *Bulbophyllum* and *Polystachya*, two genera found throughout the tropical world.

South African orchids are particularly numerous but it is the offshore islands of Madagascar, Mauritius, Réunion, and the Seychelles and Comores that contain so many species for their size. Madagascar is particularly rich, not only with fairly small-flowered species but with such spectacular plants as the long-spurred *Angraecum sesquipedale*, the chestnut-coloured *Grammangis ellisii* and the strikingly maroon-lipped and green-tepalled *Cymbidiella rhodochila*.

Mention must also be made of another group of orchids more or less confined to Africa and that is the great group of what are called 'Angraecoids'. *Angraecum* has over 200 species, many of them very small with inconspicuous green or white flowers but some such as *sesquipedale* already mentioned, *giryamae*, *comorense*, *eichleranum* and *magdalanae*. Closely related in *Aërangis* which is characterized by the long and often spiralled spurs on each flower. Of particular value in orchid collections are *Aërangis articulata* and the orange-columned *A. rhodosticta*.

Suggested plants

Aërangis
citrata, ellisii, rhodosticta, stylosa.

Ancistrochilus
rothschildianus.

Angraecopsis
gracillima.

Angraecum
eburneum, eichleranum, giryamae, infundibulare, leonis, magdalanae, scottianum, sesquiqedale, Orchidglade, Veitchii.

Ansellia
fraicana, gigantea.

Bulbophyllum
barbigerum, falcatum.

Calanthe
corymbosa.

Cirrhopetalum
umbellatum.

Cymbidiella
flabellata, humblotii, rhodochila.

Cyrtorchis
arcuata.

Disa
uniflora.

Eulophia
alta, angolensis, cucullata, horsfallii, orthoplectra, paiveana, petersii, porphyroglossa, quartiniana, steno-phylla, wakefieldii.

Eulophiella
elisabethae, roemplerana, Rolfei.

Eurychone
rothschildiana.

The genus Habenaria *includes species with beautiful, fantastic flowers, though generally they are not bright in colour. H. englerana is a ground orchid found in West Africa*

Grammangis
ellisii.

Habenaria
englerana.

Oeoniella
polystachys.

Polystachya
bella, cultriformis, tayloriana.

Vanilla
polylepsis.

Cultivation

It is not possible to give even a general guide to the cultivation of African orchids as they come from such a very wide range of climatic regimes. Some are epiphytes requiring a continuing high temperature throughout the year but others will not flower unless they are given a prolonged and dry resting phase. Some species such as *Polystachya tayloriana* will grow and flower well when treated like African succulent plants and grown alongside them.

Many of the species from east Africa need a marked diurnal contrast in their temperatures if they are to flower sucessfully: this can be achieved by installing a fan heater that can withdraw warm air in the evening and produce a rapid temperature rise as the sun comes up in the morning. Plants requiring these conditions should be separated from other orchids.

Particularly interesting to grow are the pseudo-bulbous species such as *Eulophia quartiniana* which produce so many brilliant flowers from such dull and wrinkled bulbs.

Propagation

There are over 2,500 species of orchids native to tropical and southern Africa and it would take many chapters to deal with the propagation of only the more commonly cultivated ones. However the usual techniques (see pages 58–61) can be applied with the exception of meristem culture which has been carried out on only very few African species with any degree of success.

Asiatic orchids

It was from Asia that some of the first tropical orchids were imported into Europe over two hundred years ago. Three groups of these, the Lady's Slippers, Dendrobiums and the Vandaceous types, have been dealt with in earlier chapters but there are many others just as attractive and just as easy to cultivate.

Widely grown are many species of *Coelogyne*, *Bulbophyllum*, *Cirrhopetalum* and *Calanthe*. All four genera are widespread with representative species throughout mainland Asia, its offshore islands, Australia and the Pacific. Perhaps the most easily grown are Coelogynes but all have some species available from orchid nurserymen.

Cirrhopetalum is worthy of mention as one of its species *C. umbellatulum* occurs in east Africa, Madagascar, throughout the Asiatic islands as far south as Australia and as far east as Tahiti, but, as yet, has never been found in mainland Asia. *Cirrhopetalum* flowers are unusual in that the lateral sepals are extremely elongated and usually joined along one edge. The flowers are massed in an umbel-like head and the whole structure gives a striking appearance to the plants.

Species of *Coelogyne* are deservedly popular as they can grow in very cool conditions and some such as *C. cristata* have been used as house-plants. Closely related to *Coelogyne* is the genus *Pleione* or 'Indian Crocuses' as they are popularly called. They consist of a pseudobulb from which a flower is produced. When the flower is fully developed the leaves start to grow and produce food for the pseudobulb. The pseudo-bulbs can then be lifted and stored for future planting in much the same way as ordinary crocuses or tulips.

Types Available

The list gives a selection of the more popular types.

Suggested Plants
Anoectochilus
roxburghii.

Arundina
graminifolia.

Coelogyne sanderae *is a Burmese species that was first introduced into cultivation in 1893.*

Bletilla
striata.

Bulbophyllum
beccarii, fletcheranum, fritillarifolium, grandiflorum, lobbii, macranthum, suavissimum, watsonii.

Calanthe
masuca, rosea, veratrifolia, vestita.

Cirrhopetalum
acuminatum, campanulatum, curtisii, gracillimum, makoyanum, mastersianum, medusae, rothschildianum, vaginatum.

Coelogyne
asperata, corymbosa, cristata, dayana, fimbriata, massangena, pandurata, parishii, sanderae, virescens.

Dendrochilum
cobbianum, filiforme, glumaceum.

Grammatophyllum
scriptum, speciosum.

Habenaria
radiata, rhodochila, susannae.

Phaius
flavus, tancarvilliae.

Pholidota
imbricata.

Pleione
formosana, forrestii, limiprchtii, maculata, praecox, pricei, Versailles.

Spathoglottis
aurea, ixioides, plicata.

Thunia
alba, bensoniae, marshalliana.

Cultivation and Propagation
This depends entirely on the particular plants and a specialist orchid cultivation book should be consulted. It is worth considering for outdoor cultivation the hardier members in this group.

Above left : Coelogynes are among the easiest to grow of all greenhouse orchids and Coelogyne cristata, *a Himalayan species, is perhaps the most beautiful of all orchids .*

Above right : Pleione formosana *is one of the so-called 'Indian crocuses'. The pseudobulbs are usually obtainable from non-specialist nurseries and the plants can be grown very*

easily on a windowsill and even, in mild areas, outdoors.

Opposite : Pleione praecox, *another of the 'Indian crocuses' requires rather more heat than P.* formosana *and its allies.*

CATTLEYA SKINNERI.

Appendices

Aceraherminium: *Aceras* × *Herminium* : Natural hybrid
Adaglossum: *Ada* × *Odontoglossum* : Artificial hybrid
Adioda: *Ada* × *Cochlioda* : Artificial hybrid
Aëridachnis: *Aërides* × *Arachnis* : Artificial hybrid
Aëridisia: *Aërides* × *Luisia* : Artificial hybrid
Aëriditis: *Aërides* × *Doritis* : Artificial hybrid
Aëridocentrum: *Aërides* × *Ascocentrum* : Artificial hybrid
Aëridochilus: *Aërides* × *Sarcochilus* : Artificial hybrid
Aëridofinetia: *Aërides* × *Neofinetia* (= Holcoglossum): Artificial hybrid
Aëridoglossum: *Aërides* × *Ascoglossum* : Artificial hybrid
Aëridopsis: *Aërides* × *Phalaenopsis* : Artificial hybrid
Aëridovanda: *Aërides* × *Vanda* : Artificial hybrid
Aliceara: *Brassia* × *Miltonia* × *Oncidium* : Artificial hybrid
Allenara: *Cattleya* × *Diacrium* (= Caularthron) × *Epidendrum* × *Laelia* : Artificial hybrid
Anacamptiplatanthera: *Anacamptis* × *Platanthera* : Natural hybrid
Anacamptorchis: *Anacamptis* × *Orchis* : Natural hybrid
Angraeorchis: *Angraecum* × *Cyrtorchis* : Artificial hybrid
Angrangis: *Aërangis* × *Angraecum* : Artificial hybrid
Angranthes: *Aëranthes* × *Angraecum* : Artificial hybrid
Angulocaste: *Anguloa* × *Lycaste* : Artificial hybrid
Anoectomaria: *Anoectochilus* × *Haemaria* : (= Ludisia): Artificial hybrid
Ansidium: *Ansellia* × *Cymbidium* : Artificial hybrid
Aracampe: *Acampe* × *Arachnis* : Artificial hybrid
Arachnoglossum: *Arachnis* × *Ascoglossum* : Artificial hybrid
Arachnoglottis: *Arachnis* × *Trichoglottis* : Artificial hybrid
Arachnopsis: *Arachnis* × *Phalaenopsis* : Artificial hybrid
Arachnostylis: *Arachnis* × *Rhynchostylis* : Artificial hybrid
Aranda: *Arachnis* × *Vanda* : Artificial hybrid
Aranthera: *Arachnis* × *Renanthera* : Artificial hybrid
Arizara: *Cattleya* × *Domingoa* × *Epidendrum* : Artificial hybrid
Ascandopsis: *Ascocentrum* × *Vandopsis* : Artificial hybrid
Ascocenda: *Ascocentrum* × *Vanda* : Artificial hybrid
Ascofinetia: *Ascocentrum* × *Neofinetia* (= Holcoglossum): Artificial hybrid
Asconopsis: *Ascocentrum* × *Phalaenopsis* : Artificial hybrid
Ascorachnis: *Arachnis* × *Ascocentrum* : Artificial hybrid
Ascovandoritis: *Ascocentrum* × *Doritis* × *Vanda* : Artificial hybrid
Aspasium: *Aspasia* × *Oncidium* : Artificial hybrid

Aspoglossum: *Aspasia* × *Odontoglossum* : Artificial hybrid
Bakerara: *Brassia* × *Miltonia* × *Odontoglossum* × *Oncidium* : Artificial hybrid
Barbosaara: *Cochlioda* × *Gomesa* × *Odontoglossum* × *Oncidium* : Artificial hybrid
Bardendrum: *Barkeria* × *Epidendrum* : Artificial hybrid
Barlaceras: *Aceras* × *Barlia* : Natural hybrid
Bateostylis: *Batemannia* × *Otostylis* : Artificial hybrid
Beallara: *Brassia* × *Cochlioda* × *Miltonia* × *Odontoglossum* : Artificial hybrid
Beardara: *Ascocentrum* × *Doritis* × *Phalaenopsis* : Artificial hybrid
Bishopara: *Broughtonia* × *Cattleya* × *Sophronitis* : Artificial hybrid
Bloomara: *Broughtonia* × *Laeliopsis* × *Tetramicra* : Artificial hybrid
Bokchoonara: *Arachnis* × *Ascocentrum* × *Phalaenopsis* × *Vanda* : Artificial hybrid
Bovornara: *Arachnis* × *Ascocentrum* × *Rhynchostylis* × *Vanda* : Artificial hybrid
Bradeara: *Comparettia* × *Gomesa* × *Rodriguezia* : Artificial hybrid
Brapasia: *Aspasia* × *Brassia* : Artificial hybrid
Brassada: *Ada* × *Brassia* : Artificial hybrid
Brassidium: *Brassia* × *Oncidium* : Artificial hybrid
Brassocattleya: *Brassavola* × *Cattleya* : Artificial hybrid
Brassodiacrium: *Brassavola* × *Diacrium* (= Caularthron): Artificial hybrid
Brassoepidendrum: *Brassavola* × *Epidendrum* : Artificial hybrid
Brassolaelia: *Brassavola* × *Laelia* : Artificial hybrid
Brassolaeliocattleya: *Brassavola* × *Cattleya* × *Laelia* : Artificial hybrid
Brassophronitis: *Brassavola* × *Sophronitis* : Artificial hybrid .
Brassotonia: *Brassavola* × *Broughtonia* : Artificial hybrid
Brownara: *Broughtonia* × *Cattleya* × *Diacrum* (= Caularthron): Artificial hybrid
Burkillara: *Aërides* × *Arachnis* × *Vanda* : Artificial hybrid
Burrageara: *Cochlioda* × *Miltonia* × *Odontoglossum* × *Oncidium* : Artificial hybrid
Carterara: *Aërides* × *Renanthera* × *Vandopsis* : Artificial hybrid
Catamodes: *Catasetum* × *Mormodes* : Artificial hybrid
Catanoches: *Catasetum* × *Cycnoches* : Artificial hybrid
Cattleyopsisgoa: *Cattleyopsis* × *Domingoa* : Artificial hybrid
Cattleyopsistonia: *Broughtonia* × *Cattleyopsis* : Artificial hybrid
Cattleytonia: *Broughtonia* × *Cattleya* : Artificial hybrid

Chamodenia: *Chamorchis* × *Gymnadenia* : Natural hybrid

Charlesworthara: *Cochlioda* × *Miltonia* × *Oncidium* : Artificial hybrid

Chewara: *Aërides* × *Renanthera* × *Rhynchostylis* : Artificial hybrid

Chilocentrum: *Ascocentrum* × *Chiloschista* : Artificial hybrid

Chondrobollea: *Bollea* × *Chondrorhyncha* : Artificial hybrid

Christieara: *Aërides* × *Ascocentrum* × *Vanda* : Artificial hybrid

Chuanyenara: *Arachnis* × *Renanthera* × *Rhynchostylis* : Artificial hybrid

Cleisonopsis: *Cleisocentron* × *Phalaenopsis* : Artificial hybrid

Cochella: *Cochleanthes* × *Mendoncella* : Artificial hybrid

Cochlenia: *Cochleanthes* × *Stenia* : Artificial hybrid

Coeloplatanthera: *Coeloglossum* × *Platanthera* : Natural hybrid

Colmanara: *Miltonia* × *Odontoglossum* × *Oncidium* : Artificial hybrid

Cycnodes: *Cycnoches* × *Mormodes* : Artificial hybrid

Dactylitella: *Dactylorhiza* × *Nigritella* : Natural hybrid

Dactyloglossum: *Coeloglossum* × *Dactylorhiza* : Natural hybrid

Dactylogymnadenia: *Dactylorhiza* × *Gymnadenia* : Natural hybrid

Debruyneara: *Ascocentrum* × *Luisia* × *Vanda* : Artificial hybrid

Degarmoara: *Brassia* × *Miltonia* × *Odontoglossum* : Artificial hybrid

Dekensara: *Brassavola* × *Cattleya* × *Schomburgkia* : Artificial hybrid

Devereuxara: *Ascocentrum* × *Phalaenopsis* × *Vanda* : Artificial hybrid

Diabroughtonia: *Broughtonia* × *Diacrium* (= *Caularthron*): Artificial hybrid

Diacattleya: *Cattleya* × *Diacrium* (= *Caularthron*): Artificial hybrid

Dialaelia: *Diacrium* (= *Caularthron*) × *Laelia* : Artificial hybrid

Dialaeliocattleya: *Cattleya* × *Diacrium* (= *Caularthron*) × *Laelia* : Artificial hybrid

Dialaeliopsis: *Diacrium* (= *Caularthron*) × *Laeliopsis* : Artificial hybrid

Dillonara: *Epidendrum* × *Laelia* × *Schomburgkia* : Artificial hybrid

Domindesmia: *Domingoa* × *Hexadesmia* : Artificial hybrid

Domliopsis: *Domingoa* × *Laeliopsis* : Artificial hybrid

Doricentrum: *Ascocentrum* × *Doritis* : Artificial hybrid

Doriella: *Doritis* × *Kingiella* (= Kingidium): Artificial hybrid

Doriellaopsis: *Doritis* × *Kingiella* (= Kingidium) × *Phalaenopsis* : Artificial hybrid

Dorifinetia: *Doritis* × *Neofinetia* (= Holcoglossum): Artificial hybrid

Doritaenopsis: *Doritis* × *Phalaenopsis* : Artificial hybrid

Dorthera: *Doritis* × *Renanthera* : Artificial hybrid

Dossinimaria: *Dossinia* × *Haemaria* (= Ludisia): Artificial hybrid

Downsara: *Aganisia* × *Batemannia* × *Otostylis* × *Zygosepalum* : Artificial hybrid

Durutyara: *Batemannia* × *Otostylis* × *Zygopetalum* × *Zygosepalum* : Artificial hybrid

Eastonara: *Ascocentrum* × *Gastrochilus* × *Vanda* : Artificial hybrid

Edeara: *Arachnis* × *Phalaenopsis* × *Renanthera* × *Vandopsis* : Artificial hybrid

Epibrassonitis: *Brassavola* × *Epidendrum* × *Sophronitis* : Artificial hybrid

Epicattleya: *Cattleya* × *Epidendrum* : Artificial hybrid

Epidella: *Epidendrum* × *Nageliella* : Artificial hybrid

Epidiacrium: *Diacrium* (= Caularthron) × *Epidendrum* : Artificial hybrid

Epigoa: *Domingoa* × *Epidendrum* : Artificial hybrid

Epilaelia: *Epidendrum* × *Laelia* : Artificial hybrid

Epilaeliocattleya: *Cattleya* × *Epidendrum* × *Laelia* : Artificial hybrid

Epilaeliopsis: *Epidendrum* × *Laeliopsis* : Artificial hybrid

Epiphronitis: *Epidendrum* × *Sophronitis* : Artificial hybrid

Epitonia: *Broughtonia* × *Epidendrum* : Artificial hybrid

Ernestara: *Phalaenopsis* × *Renanthera* × *Vandopsis* : Artificial hybrid

Fergusonara: *Brassavola* × *Cattleya* × *Laelia* × *Schomburgkia* × *Sophronitis* : Artificial hybrid

Forgetara: *Aspasia* × *Brassia* × *Miltonia* : Artificial hybrid

Fujioara: *Ascocentrum* × *Trichoglottis* × *Vanda* : Artificial hybrid

Fujiwarara: *Brassavola* × *Cattleya* × *Laeliopsis* : Artificial hybrid

Gastisia: *Gastrochilus* × *Luisia* : Artificial hybrid

Gastrosarcochilus: *Gastrochilus* × *Sarcochilus* : Artificial hybrid

Gauntlettara: *Broughtonia* × *Cattleyopsis* × *Laeliopsis* : Artificial hybrid

Goffara: *Luisia* × *Rhynchostylis* × *Vanda* : Artificial hybrid

Goodaleara: *Brassia* × *Cochlioda* × *Miltonia* × *Odontoglossum* × *Oncidium* : Artificial hybrid

Grammatocymbidium: *Cymbidium* × *Grammatophyllum* : Artificial hybrid

Gymnaglossum: *Coeloglossum* × *Gymnadenia* : Natural hybrid

Gymnacamptis: *Anacamptis* × *Gymnadenia* : Natural hybrid

Gymnaplatanthera: *Gymnadenia* × *Platanthera* : Natural hybrid

Gymnigritella: *Gymnadenia* × *Nigritella* : Natural hybrid

Hagerara: *Doritis* × *Phalaenopsis* × *Vanda* : Artificial hybrid

Hanesara: *Aërides* × *Arachnis* × *Neofinetia* (=Holcoglossum): Artificial hybrid

Hartara: *Broughtonia* × *Laelia* × *Sophronitis* : Artificial hybrid

Hausermannara: *Doritis* × *Phalaenopsis* × *Vandopsis* : Artificial hybrid

Hawaiiara: *Renanthera* × *Vanda* × *Vandopsis* : Artificial hybrid

Hawkesara: *Cattleya* × *Cattleyopsis* × *Epidendrum* : Artificial hybrid

Hawkinsara: *Broughtonia* × *Cattleya* × *Laelia* × *Sophronitis* : Artificial hybrid

Herbertara: *Cattleya* × *Laelia* × *Schomburgkia* × *Sophronitis* : Artificial hybrid

Hildaara: *Broughtonia* × *Laeliopsis* × *Schomb“rgkia* : Artificial hybrid

Holttumara: *Arachnis* × *Renanthera* × *Vanda* : Artificial hybrid

Hookerara: *Brassavola* × *Cattleya* × *Diacrium* (= Caularthron): Artificial hybrid

Howeara: *Leochilus* × *Oncidium* × *Rodriguezia* : Artificial hybrid

Hueylihara: *Neofinetia* × *Renanthera* × *Rhynchostylis* : Artificial hybrid

Huntleanthes: *Cochleanthes* × *Huntleya* : Artificial hybrid

Ionettia: *Comparettia* × *Ionopsis* : Artificial hybrid

Ionocidium: *Ionopsis* × *Oncidium* : Artificial hybrid

Irvingara: *Arachnis* × *Renanthera* × *Trichoglottis* : Artificial hybrid

Iwanagara: *Brassavola* × *Cattleya* × *Diacrium* (=Caularthron) × *Laelia* : Artificial hybrid

Jimenezara: *Broughtonia* × *Laelia* × *Laeliopsis* : Artificial hybrid

Joannara: *Renanthera* × *Rhynchostylis* × *Vanda* : Artificial hybrid

Kagawara: *Ascocentrum* × *Renanthera* × *Vanda* : Artificial hybrid

Kirchara: *Cattleya* × *Epidendrum* × *Laelia* × *Sophronitis* : Artificial hybrid

Komkrisara: *Ascocentrum* × *Renanthera* × *Rhynchostylis* : Artificial hybrid

Laeliocatonia: *Broughtonia* × *Cattleya* × *Laelia* : Artificial hybrid

Laeliocattkeria: *Barkeria* × *Cattleya* × *Laelia* : Artificial hybrid

Laeliocattleya: *Cattleya* × *Laelia* : Natural hybrid; Artificial hybrid

Laeliokeria: *Barkeria* × *Laelia* : Artificial hybrid

Laeliopleya: *Cattleya* × *Laeliopsis* : Artificial hybrid

Laelonia: *Broughtonia* × *Laelia* : Artificial hybrid

Lagerara: *Aspasia* × *Cochlioda* × *Odontoglossum* : Artificial hybrid

Laycockara: *Arachnis* × *Phalaenopsis* × *Vandopsis* : Artificial hybrid

Leeara: *Arachnis* × *Vanda* × *Vandopsis* : Artificial hybrid

Leocidium: *Leochilus* × *Oncidium* : Artificial hybrid

Leptolaelia: *Laelia* × *Leptotes* : Artificial hybrid

Lewisara: *Aërides* × *Arachnis* × *Ascocentrum* × *Vanda* : Artificial hybrid

Liaopsis: *Laelia* × *Laeliopsis* : Artificial hybrid

Limara: *Arachnis* × *Renanthera* × *Vandopsis* : Artificial hybrid

Lioponia: *Broughtonia* × *Laeliopsis* : Artificial hybrid

Lockochilus: *Leochilus* × *Lockhartia* : Artificial hybrid

Lowara: *Brassavola* × *Laelia* × *Sophronitis* : Artificial hybrid

Lowsonara: *Aërides* × *Ascocentrum* × *Rhynchostylis* : Artificial hybrid

Luascotia: *Ascocentrum* × *Luisia* × *Neofinetia* (= Holcoglossum): Artificial hybrid

Luinetia: *Luisia* × *Neofinetia* : (=Holcoglossum): Artificial hybrid

Luinopsis: *Luisia* × *Phalaenopsis* : Artificial hybrid

Luisanda: *Luisia* × *Vanda* : Artificial hybrid

Luivanetia: *Luisia* × *Neofinetia* (= Holcoglossum) × *Vanda* : Artificial hybrid

Lutherara: *Phalaenopsis* × *Renanthera* × *Rhynchostylis* : Artificial hybrid

Lycasteria: *Bifrenaria* × *Lycaste* : Artificial hybrid

Lymanara: *Aërides* × *Arachnis* × *Renanthera* : Artificial hybrid

Lyonara: *Cattleya* × *Laelia* × *Schomburgkia* : Artificial hybrid

Maccoyara: *Aërides* × *Vanda* × *Vandopsis* : Artificial hybrid

Macomaria: *Haemaria* (= Ludisia) × *Macodes* : Artificial hybrid

Macradesa: *Gomesa* × *Macradenia* : Artificial hybrid

Maxillacaste: *Lycaste* × *Maxillaria* : Artificial hybrid

Milpasia: *Aspasia* × *Miltonia* : Artificial hybrid

Milpilia: *Miltonia* × *Trichopilia* : Artificial hybrid

Miltassia: *Brassia* × *Miltonia* : Artificial hybrid

Miltonidium: *Miltonia* × *Oncidium* : Artificial hybrid

Miltonioda: *Cochlioda* × *Miltonia* : Artificial hybrid

Mizutara: *Cattleya* × *Diacrium* (= Caularthron) × *Schomburgkia* : Artificial hybrid

Moirara: *Phalaenopsis* × *Renanthera* × *Vanda* : Artificial hybrid

Mokara: *Arachnis* × *Ascocentrum* × *Vanda* : Artificial hybrid

Moscosoara: *Broughtonia* × *Epidendrum* × *Laeliopsis* : Artificial hybrid

Nakamotoara: *Ascocentrum* × *Neofinetia* × *Vanda* : Artificial hybrid

Nashara: *Broughtonia × Cattleyopsis × Diacrium* (=Caularthron): Artificial hybrid
Neostylis: *Neofinetia × Rhynchostylis*: Artificial hybrid
Nigrorchis: *Nigritella × Orchis*: Natural hybrid
Nobleara: *Aërides × Renanthera × Vanda*: Artificial hybrid
Northenara: *Cattleya × Epidendrum × Laelia × Schomburgkia*: Artificial hybrid
Notylidium: *Notylia × Oncidium*: Artificial hybrid
Odontioda: *Cochlioda × Odontoglossum*: Artificial hybrid
Odontobrassia: *Brassia × Odontoglossum*: Artificial hybrid
Odontocidium: *Odontoglossum × Oncidium*: Artificial hybrid
Odontonia: *Miltonia × Odontoglossum*: Artificial hybrid
Odontorettia: *Comparettia × Odontoglossum*: Artificial hybrid
Oncidenia: *Macradenia × Oncidium*: Artificial hybrid
Oncidesa: *Gomesa × Oncidium*: Artificial hybrid
Oncidettia: *Comparettia × Oncidium*: Artificial hybrid
Oncidioda: *Cochlioda × Oncidium*: Artificial hybrid
Oncidpilia: *Oncidium × Trichopilia*: Artificial hybrid
Onoara: *Ascocentrum × Renanthera × Vanda × Vandopsis*: Artificial hybrid
Opsisanda: *Vanda × Vandopsis*: Artificial hybrid
Opsistylis: *Rhynchostylis × Vandopsis*: Artificial hybrid
Orchiaceras: *Aceras × Orchis*: Natural hybrid
Orchidactyla: *Dactylorhiza × Orchis*: Natural hybrid
Orchigymnadenia: *Gymnadenia × Orchis*: Natural hybrid
Orchimantoglossum: *Himantoglossum × Orchis*: Natural hybrid
Ornithocidium: *Oncidium × Ornithophora*: Natural hybrid, Artificial hybrid
Osmentara: *Broughtonia × Cattleya × Laeliopsis*: Artificial hybrid
Otocolax: *Otostylis × Colax*: Artificial hybrid
Otonisia: *Aganisia × Otostylis*: Artificial hybrid
Otosepalum: *Otostylis × Zygosepalum*: Artificial hybrid
Palmerara: *Batemannia × Otostylis × Zygosepalum*: Artificial hybrid
Pantaapara: *Ascoglossum × Renanthera × Vanda*: Artificial hybrid
Parachilus: *Parasarochilus × Sarcochilus*: Artificial hybrid
Paulsenara: *Aërides × Arachnis × Trichoglottis*: Artificial hybrid
Pelacentrum: *Ascocentrum × Pelatantheria*: Artificial hybrid
Perreiraara: *Aërides × Rhynchostylis × Vanda*: Artificial hybrid
Pescoranthes: *Cochleanthes × Pescatorea*: Artificial hybrid
Phaiocalanthe: *Calanthe × Phaius*: Artificial hybrid

Phaiocymbidium: *Cymbidium × Phaius*: Artificial hybrid
Phalaërianda: *Aërides × Phalaenopsis × Vanda*: Artificial hybrid
Phalandopsis: *Phalaenopsis × Vandopsis*: Artificial hybrid
Phalanetia: *Neofinetia* (= Holcoglossum) × *Phalaenopsis*: Artificial hybrid
Phaliella: *Kingiella* (= Kingidium) × *Phalaenopsis*: Artificial hybrid
Phragmipaphium: *Paphiopedilum × Phragmipedium*: Artificial hybrid
Plectochilus: *Plectorrhiza × Sarcochilus*: Artificial hybrid
Pomatisia: *Luisia × Pomatocalpa*: Artificial hybrid
Potinara: *Brassavola × Cattleya × Laelia × Sophronitis*: Artificial hybrid
Propetalum: *Promenaea × Zygopetalum*: Artificial hybrid
Pseudadenia: *Gymnadenia × Pseudorchis*: Natural hybrid
Pseudinium: *Herminium × Pseudorchis*: Natural hybrid
Pseuditella: *Nigritella × Pseudorchis*: Natural hybrid
Pseudorhiza: *Dactylorhiza × Pseudorchis*: Natural hybrid
Recchara: *Brassavola × Cattleya × Laelia × Schomburgkia*: Artificial hybrid
Renades: *Aërides × Renanthera*: Artificial hybrid
Renafinanda: *Neofinetia* (= Holcoglossum) × *Renanthera × Vanda*: Artificial hybrid
Renaglottis: *Renanthera × Trichoglottis*: Artificial hybrid
Renancentrum: *Ascocentrum × Renanthera*: Artificial hybrid
Renanetia: *Neofinetia* (= Holcoglossum) × *Renanthera*: Artificial hybrid
Renanopsis: *Renanthera × Vandopsis*: Artificial hybrid
Renanstylis: *Renanthera × Rhynchostylis*: Artificial hybrid
Renantanda: *Renanthera × Vanda*: Artificial hybrid
Renanthoglossum: *Ascoglossum × Renanthera*: Artificial hybrid
Renanthopsis: *Phalaenopsis × Renanthera*: Artificial hybrid
Rhinochilus: *Rhinerrhiza × Sarcochilus*: Artificial hybrid
Rhizanthera: *Dactylorhiza × Platanthera*: Natural hybrid
Rhynchocentrum: *Ascocentrum × Rhynchostylis*: Artificial hybrid
Rhynchonopsis: *Phalaenopsis × Rhynchostylis*: Artificial hybrid
Rhynchorides: *Aërides × Rhynchostylis*: Artificial hybrid
Rhynchovanda: *Rhynchostylis × Vanda*: Artificial hybrid

Oncidium cavendishianum is a widely grown Guatemalan and Mexican species, which was first introduced into cultivation in 1835.

ONCIDIUM CAVENDISHIANUM.

Rhyndoropsis: *Doritis* × *Phalaenopsis* × *Rhynchostylis:* Artificial hybrid

Ridleyara: *Arachnis* × *Trichoglottis* × *Vanda:* Artificial hybrid

Robinara: *Aërides* × *Ascocentrum* × *Renanthera* × *Vanda:* Artificial hybrid

Rodrassia: *Brassia* × *Rodriguezia:* Artificial hybrid

Rodrettia: *Comparettia* × *Rodriguezia:* Artificial hybrid

Rodrettiopsis: *Comparettia* × *Ionopsis* × *Rodriguezia:* Artificial hybrid

Rodricidium: *Oncidium* × *Rodriguezia:* Artificial hybrid

Rodridenia: *Macradenia* × *Rodriguezia:* Artificial hybrid

Rodriglossum: *Odontoglossum* × *Rodriguezia:* Artificial hybrid

Rodriopsis: *Ionopsis* × *Rodriguezia:* Artificial hybrid

Rodritonia: *Miltonia* × *Rodriguezia:* Artificial hybrid

Rolfeara: *Brassavola* × *Cattleya* × *Sophronitis:* Artificial hybrid

Rosakirschara: *Ascocentrum* × *Neofinetia* × *Renanthera:* Artificial hybrid

Rothara: *Brassavola* × *Cattleya* × *Epidendrum* × *Laelia* × *Sophronitis:* Artificial hybrid

Rumrillara: *Ascocentrum* × *Neofinetia* × *Rhynchostylis:* Artificial hybrid

Sagarikara: *Aërides* × *Arachnis* × *Rhynchostylis:* Artificial hybrid

Sanderara: *Brassia* × *Cochlioda* × *Odontoglossum:* Artificial hybrid

Sappanara: *Arachnis* × *Phalaenopsis* × *Renanthera:* Artificial hybrid

Sarcocentrum: *Ascocentrum* × *Sarcochilus:* Artificial hybrid

Sarconopsis: *Phalaenopsis* × *Sarcochilus:* Artificial hybrid

Sarcothera: *Renanthera* × *Sarcochilus:* Artificial hybrid

Sarcovanda: *Sarcochilus* × *Vanda:* Artificial hybrid

Saridestylis: *Aërides* × *Rhynchostylis* × *Sarcanthus:* Artificial hybrid

Sartylis: *Rhynchostylis* × *Sarcochilus:* Artificial hybrid

Schafferara: *Aspasia* × *Brassia* × *Cochlioda* × *Miltonia* × *Odontoglossum:* Artificial hybrid

Schombavola: *Brassavola* × *Schomburgkia:* Artificial hybrid

Schombocattleya: *Cattleya* × *Schomburgkia:* Artificial hybrid

Schombodiacrium: *Diacrium* (= Caularthron) × *Schomburgkia:* Artificial hybrid

Schomboepidendrum: *Epidendrum* × *Schomburgkia:* Artificial hybrid

Schombolaelia: *Laelia* × *Schomburgkia:* Artificial hybrid

Schombonia: *Broughtonia* × *Schomburgkia:* Artificial hybrid

Schombonitis: *Schomburgkia* × *Sophronitis:* Artificial hybrid

Scullyara: *Cattleya* × *Epidendrum* × *Schomburgkia:* Artificial hybrid

Serapirhiza: *Dactylorhiza* × *Serapias:* Natural hybrid

Shigeuraara: *Ascocentrum* × *Ascoglossum* × *Renanthera* × *Vanda:* Artificial hybrid

Shipmanara: *Broughtonia* × *Diacrium* (= Caularthron) × *Schomburgkia:* Artificial hybrid

Sophrocattleya: *Cattleya* × *Sophronitis:* Artificial hybrid

Sophrolaelia: *Laelia* × *Sophronitis:* Artificial hybrid

Sophrolaeliocattleya: *Cattleya* × *Laelia* × *Sophronitis:* Artificial hybrid

Stacyara: *Cattleya* × *Epidendrum* × *Sophronitis:* Artificial hybrid

Stamariaara: *Ascocentrum* × *Phalaenopsis* × *Renanthera* × *Vanda:* Artificial hybrid

Stanfieldara: *Epidendrum* × *Laelia* × *Sophronitis:* Artificial hybrid

Teohara: *Arachnis* × *Renanthera* × *Vanda* × *Vandopsis:* Artificial hybrid

Tetraliopsis: *Laeliopsis* × *Tetramicra:* Artificial hybrid

Tetratonia: *Broughtonia* × *Tetramicra:* Artificial hybrid

Thesaëra: *Aërangis* × *Aëranthes:* Artificial hybrid

Trevorara: *Arachnis* × *Phalaenopsis* × *Vanda:* Artificial hybrid

Trichocidium: *Oncidium* × *Trichocentrum:* Artificial hybrid

Trichonopsis: *Phalaenopsis* × *Trichoglottis:* Artificial hybrid

Trichopsis: *Trichoglottis* × *Vandopsis:* Artificial hybrid

Trichovanda: *Trichoglottis* × *Vanda:* Artificial hybrid

Tuckerara: *Cattleya* × *Diacrium* (= Caularthron) × *Epidendrum:* Artificial hybrid

Vanalstyneara: *Miltonia* × *Odontoglossum* × *Oncidium* × *Rodriguezia:* Artificial hybrid

Vancampe: *Acampe* × *Vanda:* Artificial hybrid

Vandachnis: *Arachnis* × *Vandopsis:* Artificial hybrid

Vandaenopsis: *Phalaenopsis* × *Vanda:* Artificial hybrid

Vandewegheara: *Ascocentrum* × *Doritis* × *Phalaneopsis* × *Vanda:* Artificial hybrid

Vandofinetia: *Neofinetia* (=Holcoglossum) × *Vanda:* Artificial hybrid

Vandofinides: *Aërides* × *Neofinetia* (=Holcoglossum) × *Vanda:* Artificial hybrid

Vandopsides: *Aërides* × *Vandopsis:* Artificial hybrid

Vandoritis: *Doritis* × *Vanda:* Artificial hybrid

Vanglossum: *Ascoglossum* × *Vanda:* Artificial hybrid

Vascostylis: *Ascocentrum* × *Rhynchostylis* × *Vanda:* Artificial hybrid

Vaughnara: *Brassavola* × *Cattleya* × *Epidendrum:* Artificial hybrid

Vuylstekeara: *Cochlioda* × *Miltonia* × *Odontoglossum:* Artificial hybrid

Warneara: *Comparettia* × *Oncidium* × *Rodriguezia:* Artificial hybrid

Wilkinsara: *Ascocentrum × Vanda × Vandopsis*: Artificial hybrid

Wilsonara: *Cochlioda × Odontoglossum × Oncidium*: Artificial hybrid

Withnerara: *Aspasia × Miltonia × Odontoglossum × Oncidium*: Artificial hybrid

Yamadara: *Brassavola × Cattleya × Epidendrum × Laelia*: Artificial hybrid

Yapara: *Phalaenopsis × Rhynchostylis × Vanda*: Artificial hybrid

Yoneoara: *Renanthera × Rhynchostylis × Vandopsis*: Artificial hybrid

Yusofara: *Arachnis × Ascocentrum × Renanthera × Vanda*: Artificial hybrid

Zygobatemannia: *Batemannia × Zygopetalum*: Artificial hybrid

Zygocaste: *Lycaste × Zygopetalum*: Artificial hybrid

Zygocella: *Mendoncella × Zygopetalum*: Artificial hybrid

Zygocolax: *Colax × Zygopetalum*: Artificial hybrid

Zygonisia: *Aganisia × Zygopetalum*: Artificial hybrid

Zygorhyncha: *Chondrorhyncha × Zygopetalum*: Artificial hybrid

Zygostylis: *Otostylis × Zygopetalum*: Artificial hybrid

LÆLIA AUTUMNALIS.

Arranged according to sub-tribes and including only those genera of which one or more species are cultivated.

Cypripediinae
Cypripedium : North Temperate
Selenipedilinae
Selenipedium : Tropical America
Phragmipedilinae
Phragmipedium : Tropical America
Paphiopedilinae
Paphiopedilum : Tropical Asia, Pacific Islands
Orchidinae
Pecteilis : Tropical Asia; *Stenoglottis :* Tropical Africa, South Africa; *Cynorkis :* Tropical and South Africa, Madagascar; *Habenaria :* Pan-tropical, Australasia; *Bonatea :* Tropical and South Africa, Arabia; *Brachycorythis :* Palaeotropical; *Platanthera :* North Temperate, Tropical Asia and Tropical America; *Ophrys :* Europe, Mediterranean; *Serapias :* Mediterranean; *Himantoglossum :* Europe, Mediterranean; *Anacamptis :* Europe, Mediterranean; *Aceras :* Europe, Mediterranean, Temperate Asia; *Orchis :* Europe, Mediterranean, Temperate Asia; *Dactylorhiza :* North Temperate, Mediterranean
Disinae
Disa : Tropical and South Africa, Madagascar
Satyriinae
Satyrium : Tropical and South Africa, Madagascar
Diuridinae
Diuris : Tropical Asia, Australasia
Pterostylidinae
Pterostylis : Tropical Asia, Australasia, Pacific Islands
Glomerinae
Mediocalcar : Tropical Asia, Pacific Islands; *Epiblastus :* Tropical Asia, Pacific Islands; *Agrostophyllum :* Mascarene Islands, Tropical Asia, Pacific Islands
Podochilinae
Appendicula : Tropical Asia, Pacific Islands
Sobraliinae
Sobralia : Tropical America
Arethusinae
Bletilla : Tropical and Temperate Asia
Vanillinae
Vanilla : Pan-Tropical
Spiranthinae
Spiranthes : Cosmopolitan excl. Tropical America, Tropical Africa, South Africa and Madagascar; *Cyclopogon :* Tropical America, Temperate South America; *Pelexia :* Tropical America, Temperate South America;

In its native country the Mexican species Laelia autumnalis *has been used as a cough cure but in the rest of the world it is a very popular greenhouse subject.*

Stenorrhynchos : Temperate North, Tropical and Temperate South America
Elleanthinae
Elleanthus : Tropical America
Erythrodinae
Goodyera : North Temperate, Madagascar, Tropical Asia, Australasia, Pacific Islands; *Erythrodes :* Temperate North, South and Tropical America, Tropical Asia, Pacific Islands; *Dossinia :* Tropical Asia; *Macodes :* Tropical Asia, Pacific Islands; *Ludisia :* Tropical Asia; *Zeuxine :* Palaeotropical, Australasia; *Anoectochilus :* Tropical Asia, Australasia, Pacific Islands
Bletiinae
Phaius : Palaeotropical, Australasia; *Calanthe :* Pan-tropical, Australasia; *Chysis :* Tropical America; *Spathoglottis :* Tropical Asia, Australasia, Pacific Islands; *Bletia :* Tropical America; *Coelia :* Tropical America
Liparidinae
Malaxis : Cosmopolitan; *Oberonia :* Palaeotropical, Australasia; *Liparis :* Cosmopolitan excl. New Zealand
Thuniinae
Arundina : Tropical Asia, Pacific Islands; *Thunia :* Tropical Asia

Pleurothallidinae
Masdevallia : Tropical America; *Lepanthes :* Tropical America; *Platystele :* Tropical America; *Pleurothallis :* Tropical America; *Lepanthopsis :* Tropical America; *Restrepia :* Tropical America; *Stelis :* Tropical America
Dendrobiinae
Cadetia : Tropical Asia, Australasia, Pacific Islands
Dendrobium : Tropical Asia, Australasia, Pacific Islands
Ephemerantha : Tropical Asia, Australasia, Pacific Islands
Epigeneium : Tropical Asia; *Diplocaulobium :* Tropical Asia, Australasia, Pacific Islands; *Eria :* Tropical Asia, Australasia, Pacific Islands; *Trichotosia :* Tropical Asia, Pacific Islands; *Porpax :* Tropical Asia; *Cryptochilus :* Tropical Asia
Laeliinae
Epidendrum : Tropical America; *Alamania :* Tropical America; *Barkeria :* Tropical America; *Lanium :* Tropical America; *Caularthron :* Tropical America; *Encyclia :* Tropical America; *Cattleya :* Tropical America; *Laelia :* Tropical America; *Rhyncholaelia :* Tropical America; *Brassavola :* Tropical America; *Schomburgkia :* Tropical America; *Tetramicra :* Tropical America; *Neocogniauxia :* Tropical America; *Sophronitis :* Tropical America; *Sophronitella :* Tropical America; *Broughtonia :* Tropical

America; *Laeliopsis :* Tropical America; *Cattleyopsis :* Tropical America; *Isabelia :* Tropical America; *Leptotes :* Tropical America; *Isochilus :* Tropical America;

Jacquiniella : Tropical America; *Ponera* : Tropical America; *Nageliella* : Tropical America; *Arpophyllum* : Tropical America; *Domingoa* : Tropical America; *Scaphyglottis* : Tropical America; *Hexadesmia* : Tropical America

Coelogyninae
Coelogyne : Tropical Asia, Pacific Islands; *Pleione* : Tropical Asia; *Dendrochilum* : Tropical Asia

Bulbophyllinae
Bulbophyllum : Pan-tropical, Australasia; *Cirrhopetalum* : Palaeotropical, Australasia

Polystachyinae
Ansellia : Tropical Africa; *Polystachya* : Pan-tropical

Cyrtopodiinae
Geodorum : Tropical Asia, Australasia, Pacific Islands; *Cyrtopodium* : Tropical America; *Warrea* : Tropical America; *Eulophia* : Pan-tropical, Australasia; *Graphorkis* : Tropical Africa, Madagascar; *Eulophiella* : Madagascar; *Eulophidium* : Pan-tropical

Cymbidiinae
Dipodium : Tropical Asia, Australasia, Pacific Islands
Cymbidium : Tropical Asia, Australasia
Grammatophyllum : Tropical Asia, Pacific Islands
Grammangis : Madagascar; *Cymbidiella* : Madagascar

Maxillariinae
Mormolyca : Tropical America; *Trigonidium* : Tropical America; *Ornithidium* : Tropical America; *Scuticaria* : Tropical America : *Maxillaria* : Tropical America

Cryptocentrinae
Cryptocentrum : Tropical America

Lycastinae
Xylobium : Tropical America; *Bifrenaria* : Tropical America; *Teuscheria* : Tropical America; *Lycaste* : Tropical America; *Anguloa* : Tropical America

Zygopetalinae
Aganisia : Tropical America; *Colax* : Tropical America; *Zygopetalum* : Tropical America; *Zygosepalum* : Tropical America; *Mendoncella* : Tropical America; *Batemannia* : Tropical America; *Promenaea* : Tropical America; *Warreella* : Tropical America

Huntleyinae
Stenia : Tropical America; *Chondrorhyncha* : Tropical America; *Cochleanthes* : Tropical America; *Pescatoria* : Tropical America; *Bollea* : Tropical America; *Huntleya* : Tropical America

Stanhopeinae
Sievekingia : Tropical America; *Polycycnis* : Tropical America; *Stanhopea* : Tropical America; *Gongora* : Tropical America; *Coryanthes* : Tropical America

Notyliinae
Notylia : Tropical America; *Macradenia* : Tropical America

Oncidiinae
Lockhartia : Tropical America; *Gomesa* : Tropical America; *Rodrigueziella* : Tropical America;

Osmoglossum : Tropical America; *Odontoglossum* : Tropical America; *Symphyglossum* : Tropical America; *Aspasia* : Tropical America; *Ada* : Tropical America; *Brassia* : Tropical America; *Miltonia* : Tropical America; *Oncidium* : Tropical America; *Cyrtochilum* : Tropical America; *Leochilus* : Tropical America; *Sigmatostalix* : Tropical America; *Ornithophora* : Tropical America

Trichopiliinae
Trichopilia : Tropical America; *Cochlioda* : Tropical America

Comparettiinae
Rodriguezia : Tropical America; *Comparettia* : Tropical America

Catasetinae
Mormodes : Tropical America; *Catasetum* : Tropical America; *Cycnoches* : Tropical America

Aëridinae
Thrixspermum : Tropical Asia, Australasia, Pacific Islands; *Rhinerrhiza* : Australasia; *Ornithochilus* : Tropical Asia; *Aërides* : Tropical Asia; *Doritis* : Tropical Asia; *Phalaenopsis* : Tropical Asia, Australasia; *Kingidium* : Tropical Asia

Vandinae
Luisia : Tropical Asia, Australasia, Pacific Islands; *Vanda* : Tropical Asia, Australasia, Pacific Islands; *Euanthe* : Tropical Asia; *Esmeralda* : Tropical Asia; *Vandopsis* : Tropical Asia, Pacific Islands; *Arachnis* : Tropical Asia; *Armodorum* : Tropical Asia; *Renanthera* : Tropical Asia, Pacific Islands; *Renantherella* : Tropical Asia; *Ascoglossum* : Tropical Asia, Pacific Islands; *Ascocentrum* : Tropical Asia; *Cleisocentron* : Tropical Asia

Sarcanthinae
Saccolabium : Tropical Asia, Australasia; *Gastrochilus* : Tropical Asia; *Holcoglossum* : Tropical Asia; *Neofinetia* : Tropical Asia; *Acampe* : Palaeotropical; *Malleola* : Tropical Asia; *Robiquetia* : Tropical Asia, Australasia, Pacific Islands; *Plectrorrhiza* : Australasia; *Schoenorchis* : Tropical Asia, Australasia, Pacific Islands; *Sarcanthus* : Tropical Asia, Australasia; *Camarotis* : Tropical Asia, Australasia, Pacific Islands; *Pomatocalpa* : Tropical Asia, Australasia, Pacific Islands; *Trichoglottis* : Tropical Asia, Pacific Islands

Podanginae
Aëranthes : Madagascar

Angraecinae
Angraecum : Tropical and South Africa, Madagascar, Tropical Asia

Aërangidinae
Diaphananthe : Tropical Africa; *Bolusiella* : Tropical Africa; *Plectrelminthus* : Tropical Africa, Madagascar; *Aërangis* : Tropical and South Africa, Madagascar; *Rangaëris* : Tropical and South Africa; *Mystacidium* : Tropical and South Africa; *Cyrtorchis* : Tropical and South Africa; *Ancistrorhynchus* : Tropical Africa; *Tridactyle* : Tropical and South Africa

Appendix C: List of Orchid Societies

This is not a complete listing but gives a range of the societies that publicize their activities. For the correct up-to-date addresses of society offices or secretaries, the national orchid societies or orchid councils or the national orchid journals should be consulted. The American Orchid Society, c/o Botanical Museum, Harvard University, Cambridge, Massachusetts 02138, United States of America, will provide the address of most affiliated societies, and their Annual Yearbook should be consulted. Most commercial orchid nurseries will be in touch with local and national orchid societies and can give you their addresses.

Australia: Australian Orchid Council (representing all State orchid societies)
Austria: Osterreichische Orchideen-Gesellschaft
Bahamas: Orchid Society of Bahamas
Barbados: Barbados Orchid Circle
Brazil: Sociedade Brasileira do Orquidofilos
Brunei: Brunei State Orchid Society
Colombia: Sociedad Colombiana de Orquideologia
Czechoslovakia: Club der Orchideenfreunde in Prag
Denmark: Dansk Orchide Club
France: Societe Francaise d'Orchidophilie
Germany: (Federal Republic): Deutsche Orchideen-Gesellschaft E.V.
Haiti: Orchid Society of Haiti
Hawaii: Hawaiian Orchid Societies Inc.
Holland: Nederlandse Orchideen Vereniging
Italy: Associazione Italiana per la Orchidee
Jamaica: Jamaica Orchid Society
Japan: Japan Orchid Society
Kenya: Kenya Orchid Society
Malaysia and Singapore: Orchid Society of South-East Asia

Mexico: Sociedad Orquidofila de Guadalajara
New Zealand: New Zealand Orchid Society
Peru: Orchid Society of Peru
Philippines: Philippine Orchid Society
Rhodesia: Rhodesian Orchid Society
South Africa: South African Orchid Council (representing all South African Orchid societies)
Sri Lanka: Orchid Circle of Sri Lanka
Sweden: Orchid Club of Stockholm
Switzerland: Schweizerische Orchideengesellschaft
Taiwan: Taiwan Orchid Society
Thailand: Orchid Society of Thailand
Trinidad: Trinidad Orchid Society
United Kingdom: British Orchid Council; Birmingham and Midland Orchid Society; Bournemouth, Poole and District Orchid Society; Bristol and West of England Orchid Society; British Orchid Growers' Association (Trade members only); Cambridge and District Orchid Society; Central Orchid Society; Cheltenham and District Orchid Society; Cheshire and North Wales Orchid Society; Devon Orchid Society; Medway and District Discussion Group (of OSGB); North of England Orchid Society; Orchid Society of East Anglia; Orchid Society of Great Britain; Royal Horticultural Society (the premier awarding and judging society for all plants); Scottish Orchid Society; Sheffield and South Yorkshire Orchid Society; Solihull and District Orchid Society; South Wales and Monmouthshire Orchid Society; Thames Valley Orchid Society; Wessex Orchid Society
United States of America: Cymbidium Society of America; International Phalaenopsis Society of America; The American Orchid Society
Venezuela: Sociedad de Orquideologia de Carabobo

England: *London*, Kew: Royal Botanic Gardens; *Oxford*: University Botanic Garden; *Surrey, Wisley*: Royal Horticultural Society's Garden
Scotland: *Edinburgh*: Royal Botanic Garden; *Glasgow*: Botanic Gardens
Ireland: *Dublin*: National Botanic Gardens
Australia: *Sydney*: Royal Botanic Gardens
Brazil: *Rio de Janeiro*: Jardim Botanico do Rio de Janeiro; *Sao Paulo*: Jardim Botanico de Sao Paulo
Canada: *Montreal*: Montreal Botanical Garden
Denmark: *Copenhagen*: University Botanic Garden
Fiji: *Suva*: Suva Gardens
France: *Paris*: Jardin des Plantes
Germany: *Berlin*: Botanischer Garten und Museum; *Frankfurt*: Palmergarten
Holland: *Leiden*: University Botanic Garden
Indonesia: *Bogor*: Kebun Roya Indonesia

Madagascar: *Tananarive*: Jardin Botanique
Malaysia: *Penang*: Botanic Gardens
New Zealand: *Christchurch*: Christchurch Botanic Gardens
Nigeria: *Ife*: University Botanical Gardens
Portugal: *Coimbra*: Jardim Botânico da Faculdade de Ciencias da Universidade de Coimbra
Singapore: *Singapore*: Botanic Gardens
Sri Lanka: *Peradeniya*: Royal Botanic Gardens
Sweden: *Göteborg*: Göteborgs Botaniska Trödgården
U.S.S.R.: *Leningrad*: Komarov Botanical Institute Garden
U.S.A.: *Berkeley*: University of California Botanical Garden; *Brooklyn*: Brooklyn Botanic Garden; *Honolulu*: Foster Botanical Garden; *New York*: New York Botanical Garden; *St. Louis*: Missouri Botanical Garden

Index

LISSOHILUS

168

Index

Page numbers in italics refer to illustrations. Species and hybrids listed in the chapter Orchids for the Amateur Grower have not been listed separately in the index.

Eulophia horsfallii, *formerly known as* Lissochilus roseus, *is an African terrestrial well worth cultivating.*